IRELAND OBSERVED

MAY VEBER

Translated from the French by Jean Joss

GALLERY BOOKS
An Imprint of W. H. Smith Publishers Inc.
112 Maddison Avenue
New York City 10016

This edition published 1986 for USA, Canada and the Philippines by Gallery Books, an imprint of W. H. Smith Publishers Inc., 112 Madison Avenue, New York, NY 10016.

First published 1980 by Hachette.
Published 1980 in Great Britain by Kaye & Ward Ltd, London.
Published 1980 in the USA by Oxford University Press Inc., New York.

ISBN 0-8317-4997-0

Design by Jean-Louis Germain. Printed in Italy by Milanostampa - Farigliano (Cuneo)

Contents

1 Dublin

The Emerald Isle, famous for its unpredictable nature, begins here among the subtle tints of a uniformly grey landscape, pierced only by the cries of the soaring gulls; here on the east coast, where its capital city stretches out along the bay like some tangible sketch in charcoals. The simple grey is relieved by varying tones of pearl, of slate, of mouse-grey, of cinder and iron, and here, where the eye reaches infinity, it changes and dissolves into the distant, muffled, intangible sounds of the city which surge through and melt into the drizzling rain. Dubh-Linn, the Dark Pool, is as dark as the waters of the **Liffey**, which only a short time ago took their hue from the peat beds below. James Joyce, its spiritual son, whose writings im-

mortalised Dublin for all time, described it as a 'gloomy, foggy, city'. Certainly Joyce, with his baffling ambiguity, was a true Dubliner, a modern hero of Erin, long disowned by his own people. Here it is difficult to elude his formidable presence, difficult to avoid looking through his eyes and following step by step the paths already taken by Stephen Dedalus and Leopold Bloom. It is almost impossible to extricate oneself from literary images. The Dublin of the 1900s was able to bask with impunity in the fullness of its past; even today the style of its buildings (and, indeed, the people themselves behind the dark brick walls) hardly seems to have changed. Joyce, who left Dublin at the age of 20, never to return, knew the city's streets better than anyone; their intimate geography was indelibly stamped in his memory. Dublin, with its thousand faces, was the sole subject of all his writings, the immortal Ithaca of his novel *Ulysses*. The author, Camille Bourniquel, observed that, 'Even in exile Joyce retained the remembrance of these places and the minutest details of the life there. His vision was both vengeful and nostalgic; in it realism alternated with mythology. It was the true setting of his work, completely recreated and given a new existence. . . .' Joyce has enshrined Dublin for ever as a bittersweet city, a strange maze of trembling

The docks on the Liffey estuary.

The new Ireland. Thanks to the economic 'miracle' the country is no longer forced to live in isolation.

plaintive voice of an old woman haunted by memories. The pavements are soon swarming with a nonchalant, chattering crowd which is blurred by the drizzling rain and absorbed into its fine web.

The metropolis takes you by surprise straight away, tucked in the middle of the island's fertile greenness. It seems strange in this small country of wide, grassy expanses swept by the Atlantic winds. Such a city appears as one of those incongruities, one of the dark sides of the country. Joyce has already called attention to Dublin's 'morose enormity'. It is, though, only a relative enormity as the city today contains only some seven hundred thousand citizens out of the mere seven million in the whole of the Republic of Ireland. It also contains 40 per cent of the country's industry and produces more than half of the national income. In a country that is determinedly rural such a city resembles an over-large head, or a malignant growth, placed there through the whims of fate. Or, to be more accurate, through the caprices of the powers who have occupied it since its origins. It was the

mists; a city he both adored and damned and which he portrayed again and again in his writings. Indeed, he claimed (and not as an idle boast) that if by chance Dublin was destroyed, anyone at all could rebuild it by using his narratives.

The clouds pass over in shades of grey-white and grey-black into the paleness of the far west. The bridges across the Liffey are alive with a multitude of bicycles. The small newspaper-sellers, tattered urchins, who look as though they have come straight from the pages of a Dickensian novel, spread through the wet streets shouting the day's headlines at the tops of their voices. A **harpist** wearily picks out the melancholy notes of a ballad that harks back to ancestral woes, like the muffled,

The last remaining street harpists.

O'Meara's, a pub of a hundred years standing, frequented by several generations of patriots.

Vikings who first founded the city in the ninth century, that far-off era of fire and blood. It began as a simple assemblage of forts, a nest for these pirates of the cold northlands and was swiftly transformed into a base from which they could hold the rich islanders to ransom in a more leisurely fashion. The English occupation came next with the advent of Henry II in 1172 when the Plantagenet made it his principal base and the capital of the Pale.

Dublin then has a foreign air, since the predominantly rural Irish did not build cities. And Dublin appears to be English, too, with its ancient castle bearing witness to the years of the Ascendancy when London and its English land-lords ruled over the country. There is nothing, at first sight, that is very Irish about this city. The illusion that one could be in London is total; there are squares and greens of impeccable turf set with deckchairs, all in the English tradition. In the better areas the severe lines of the Georgian architecture could well grace London's West End; in the less salubrious areas the gloomy, leprous slums (albeit fast disappearing) recall the Victorian East End; in dockland it could well be the Thames beyond Tower Bridge; along O'Connell Street, Westmoreland Street or Dame Street it conjures up a mélange of Westminster and the City leading into Soho. Double-decker buses throng nose to tail in the streets, though these are painted green (the colour of independent Ireland), not red like their London counterparts. And then, gradually, one becomes aware of a whole range of subtle but undeniable differences. Dublin may possess the history of an English city and also bear a strong resemblance to one, gained through more than eight centuries of close association, but appearances, as ever, prove deceptive. Dublin is in fact, by some alchemy known only to the men of Erin, the most intrinsically 'Irish' city of all. It was the cradle of Swift, Sterne, Sheridan, Wilde, Shaw, Synge, Yeats, O'Casey and Joyce, names to conjure with in the foremost literary circles on the other side of the channel, despite the poverty of their literary background. Yet, like their countrymen, these writers were able to inhabit two worlds and they easily managed to shrug off the London influence. So the setting here may resemble that of an English stage, but the Dubliners themselves are remarkable actors and not one of them would meet with his double in the real London. Once you are across St George's Channel you are truly in a different world.

This new world begins with the shop fronts bearing such names as O'Hara, O'Neill, O'Flaherty, Kelly, Mahony, Fogarty, Kennedy, Fitzpatrick, Kavanagh, Ryan, Donovan, Lenehan, Moynihan. It continues in the streets around **St Stephen's Green** or on the banks of the Liffey, which is the city's pivot, cutting it into two with its bustling, teeming traffic. For those who know where to look the pavements of Dublin present an astonishing palette of humanity, one of the most unusual in Europe. The Irish capital has a popula-

The capital for beer, be it black, brown, golden or russet.

A pub on the bank of the Grand Canal, typical of the unobtrusive charm of the northern cities.

The Liffey, between Halfpenny Bridge and the dome of the Four Courts.

The young person's Ireland — folk music and the inevitable game of darts.

tion unlike any other; it has even been said that Dublin nurtures 'the greatest menagerie of eccentrics in the western world'. Perhaps this is because Dublin remains essentially a port and because, as such, it is a natural meeting-place for strange worlds. But most of all, it is because this city holds the intrinsic essence of Ireland itself, forming a unique microcosm where non-conformity is second nature. All you have to do to convince yourself that this is true is to watch the people of Dublin as they pass by and their unusual character will demand your attention. Simultaneously the scene will disclose members of the fallen nobility, dressed in threadbare tweeds, well-preserved remains of the one-time Anglo-Irish ruling class; a plethora of priests and nuns, row upon row of them, their traditional costume mingling with the modern-day fashions; numbers of bearded and long-haired youths with florid complexions and the dreaming expressions of bards or prophets of the Celtic revival; a few straight-laced gentlemen in frock-coats, steeped in the respectability of a bygone age; extravagantly dressed dowagers; feverish, turbulent, perspiring and unashamedly rowdy gypsyfolk; jovial tramps and so on. . . . And then there is the simple man in the street who has obviously not long been uprooted from his native peat. He is clad in indefinable style (scorning the well-creased British trousers) and crowned with the traditional and inevitably crumpled cloth cap. He has a long, angular face with huge, sad eyes reflecting in turn all the bitterness and resignation in the world. Here, with unemployment at the exceptionally high level of 12 per cent, they play out a scene from *Waiting for Godot*, in their own free and natural adaptation, every day that God sends. And, as the saying goes, when God created time, He created enough of it. . . .

Destinies entwine here. The indolent Dublin is where the many faces of

Ireland meet – Ireland the gay, the gloomy, the indigent, the opulent, the quarrelsome, the tight-fisted, the lavish, the open, the secret; each showing its own great vitality. Over the last decade the population has increased by 13 per cent. That more

than half of it is under the age of 25 is not difficult to believe when you see the swarms of laughing children rushing round the streets. (According to one sociologist, the Catholic couples in Dublin have the highest fertility record of any western city!) And let

Soliloquizing in front of a Guinness: waiting for Godot. . . .

A scene from the recent production of *The Silver Tassie* by Sean O'Casey, 1928, at the Abbey Theatre.

packed with drinkers, its woodwork showing the patina of age and its brass giving it a shining warmth, provides an ideal setting for indulging in this major activity. The intellectual, artistic and political life of Dublin owes much to the pub and is inextricably linked to it.

From the oldest ('The Brazen Head' dating from 1666) to the newest, from the smartest to the most sordid, music plays an important role, as does poetry. These are not merely the prerogative of the singing pubs and the ballad clubs. And as round follows round, nothing can equal another pint for helping to keep the singing going or for solving the world's problems. As a rule strangers participate with good grace; after all you cannot raise your glasses with these sons of the soil and remain strangers for long! There are those who will tell you that the pubs aren't what they used to be, since women have been allowed in them for some time now!

A shrine worked in bronze containing the Bell of St Patrick, end of the eleventh century (National Museum of Ireland).

us not forget to mention that this city also encapsulates the legendary Ireland of that other great Dubliner, Brendan Behan, the Ireland which has an unquenchable thirst and is full of amazing drunkards. The capital is rich in pubs and would be unimaginable without Mulligan's, Neary's, O'Donoghue's, McDaid's, Kehoe's, The Long Hall, The Stag's Head and other justly famous institutions. The list is inexhaustible. The authors of one excellent little guide to Ireland, wrote that, 'No-one has yet been able to count the exact number of pubs there are in Dublin. Some say a thousand, but no-one knows whether they were seeing double or if their powers of observation failed them before they could complete their enquiries!' The **Dublin publand** is its own strange and quaint world. During opening time stout and whiskey flow freely, as does conversation in the inimitable Irish accent with its lilting slowness. Talk is important in Dublin life and the smoke-filled pub, jam-

Trinity College Library: the Thomas Burgh library begun in 1712, where the famous illuminated manuscripts are displayed.

The world's most beautiful manuscript the Book of Kells, about 800. St John page 291. (Trinity College Library.)

13

The quiet man:
between Jesus, stout
and the tote.

But folklore and civilising influences apart, the pub stands up well to the assaults of the modern day. Together with the church it is still one of the pillars of Irish society. There is, of course, the matchless pleasure of talking and after all 'Guinness is good for into space or staring darkly into the black depths of his Guinness, he lets himself sink back into the stream of past dramas, attempting to drown his sorrows at the bottom of a tankard of this velvety and bitter brew; as bitter as his sorrow which goes back far the guffaws of Christy Mahon, the western world's buffoon, the outraged cries of *The Plough and the Stars*. Words provided a means of escape from a secular solitude, or affirmed a desperate revolt, or explained the hard life of an oppressed race; words usually

Guinness's Brewery: the largest brewery in Europe, founded in 1759, exports to 120 countries.

you', as everyone knows! But for the devotee the pub remains hallowed ground, providing a cheap means of escape, a refuge from the harsh realities of everyday life. Because the Irishman is at once loquacious and taciturn, ultra-gay and ultra-melancholy; he can get drunk with words or remain stubbornly silent. He is certainly fond of eloquent speaking, but he also has a prodigious memory and often he is content to allow that to speak for him. In silence, with eyes gazing vacantly beyond yesterday. . . .

Here the cruelty of fate is always put into words and pictures, repeated and resifted until it is hardly bearable. After the pub, the theatre provides the other ideal outlet for the telling of tales and for the unleashing of emotions. The greatest of these is the famous **Abbey Theatre** which saw the first flickering of the renaissance of modern Ireland at the dawn of this century. The birth took place through the lamentations of *Deirdre of the Sorrows*, controlled by a savage black humour, the famous Irish wit which knows no equal. The Dubliner, like every son of Erin, knows the plot by heart. Firstly it is the tide of history, secondly his own misery. Though the first has now been deflected (apart from the question of Ulster), the second has by no means completely disappeared. One has only to explore certain of the worst districts in the capital to come face to face with naked poverty.

Here are stinking little hovels, their facades faded and running with damp, their windows black with dirt, their walls sticky with filth: a wasteland showing the still-open wounds of recent poverty as well as the scabs and scars of the bloody civil war years. It remains a blot upon the city although it is, thankfully, no longer the Dante's Inferno that foreign visitors to Dublin encountered at the end of the last century, when the city boasted one of the highest density slum areas in the whole of Europe. The consumer society is gaining ground rapidly, even on this island that has been relatively isolated for so long, but Dublin nevertheless remains, in the words of novelist Edna O'Brien, 'The most pleasant city to live in, if you are poor.' It has a split personality, this city, with its atmosphere charged by an undying awareness of the past, because gloomy, chilly Dublin with the dilapidated houses and shabby streets is also resplendent Dublin, rich in fabled cultural treasures of a fascinating race. The perfect example of this is the Book of Kells, symbolic of the island's very soul and steeped in a dreamlike quaintness, the legacy of ancient writers and men of God.

The Irish, who vowed an unshakable devotion to the Almighty more than 15 centuries ago, and who remain the most passionate members of the faithful, have, nonetheless, new preoccupations these days. The chief is how to raise their standard of living. And so, although replicas of the Sacred Heart, St Teresa and the Child Jesus continue to be sold in the religious shops and department stores, it is the daily export figures for Guinness (some five million bottles per day) that have taken on a deep significance for today and which are bringing a certain amount of prosperity to Eire. Despite the progress of the secular and the consumer society, which some say has 'created an environment hostile to the survival of true religion', it is worth remembering that 90 per cent of the Irish are still practising Catholics. As a result, there is a Protestant minority.

Partition rears its ugly head even here. Dublin itself has no less than three cathedrals; two are Anglican, St Patrick's and Christ Church; the Catholic St Mary's is the one most often missed by the visitor. All three are the gloomy products of the nineteenth century, all equally neat, chilly and soulless, surprising in this fervently religious country. Religious intolerance here, too, is sadly long-lived; it was only in 1973 that the ban on Catholics entering Christ Church was officially lifted.

Christ Church is the oldest of the two historic cathedrals, founded around the year 1000 by Dunan, the first bishop of Dublin and the Norwegian king Sigtryggr. Within its walls lies the heart of St Laurence O'Toole, the patron saint of Dublin. It also contains a tomb with a carved effigy said to be that of the notorious Strongbow (Richard Clare, Earl of Pembroke), who with his Anglo-Norman barons took

Dublin by a surprise attack in 1170. St Patrick's, consecrated in 1192 is even richer in memories, underlying the dusty banners and standards displayed there. The indomitable Jonathan Swift, creator of Gulliver, was Dean here for 32 years. When he died in 1745 he was buried at the side of the mysterious 'Stella', Esther Johnson, whom he had loved with desperate devotion for most of his life. Swift wrote his own epitaph: 'He is laid where bitter rage can no more tear his heart.' He was the author of vitriolic pamphlets against the English, pitting himself against the dictum that 'might is right', and was undoubtedly the first to develop and refine that savage, satirical humour which subsequently became the literary mode for writers in exile. The most pointed use of this was in his *Modest Proposal for Preventing the Children of Ireland from being a Burden to their Parents or Country* . . . written in 1729 and in which he advocated that the hordes of starv-

'Let there be life.' (James Joyce)

16

God and morality and religion come first.' (James Joyce)

ing children wandering round the city streets should be eaten while still young and tender, 'stewed, roasted, baked or boiled . . . in a fricassee or a ragoût' so that they would avoid becoming victims of famine!

Dublin also has two universities. One is the Catholic University College; the other, the famous **Trinity College**, is very much older. This was founded by the royal charter of Elizabeth I in 1591 for the express purpose of combatting 'the papist influence' and was to become the nursery of the Humanities in this 'uncivilised, isolated and ignorant country'. Even in the twentieth century it has remained a bastion of Protestantism and Puritanism. It is also a bastion of culture as the quality of its alumni well illustrates and a great number of eminent scholars enter its portals daily. Here, too, Catholics had to wait for the more liberal attitudes of the seventies before their students (who have been ad-

Individualism amid the uniformity of brick. . . .

. . . The Georgian front doors painted in all colours.

as examples of an exquisite and distinguished obsolescence. This refined and sophisticated architecture was classed as Georgian because it was born in the reigns of the four Georges, and it is this which gives the city its original character. Palladio was given the accolade; his designs were taken and adapted along the banks of the Liffey. First it was the left bank in the north, then the southern right

mitted since 1873 and nowadays form a large majority) were allowed to enrol here without individual permission from their bishop.

The district which contains the cathedrals is the oldest part of Dublin, being its original nucleus which developed within the protection of the city walls. Apart from these holy places the capital has very little to offer in the way of buildings which pre-date 1700. It was not until the Age of Enlightenment that the mediaeval aspect of this small fortified town changed, making it into one of the most beautiful of European cities and a dynamic cultural capital, seething with life. It was at this great moment in its history that Dublin put on the mantle of a true capital city.

After the nightmare rule of the Cromwellian period, Dublin suddenly entered a lull in its stormy history. A relatively stable political scene opened up, to be soon followed by an unprecedented prosperity. A new ruling class came to power, the Protestant landlords of the Anglo-Irish Ascendancy, who owed their supremacy to the victory won by William of Orange. These rich aristocrats were a small minority but they were cultured men who had travelled throughout Europe and who wished to take part in the great movement towards the Enlightenment. They wanted their city to be up-to-date and so they called on the greatest architects, particularly those from England and Italy, the best sculptors and decorators of the period. The renovation was total and the city of Dublin began to live and move in a more noble fashion.

The streets became more open, due in part to the meticulous and imaginative work of the Wide Street Commissioners. Elegant bridges began to span the Liffey and the Grand Canal – Queen's Bridge, Sarah Bridge, Huband Bridge. Dublin was decked with public buildings and private town houses, particularly in the second half of the century. Despite demolition and development since, many remain

bank which swiftly became the areas where it was fashionable to build and to reside. Antiquity lived again! The Dublin buildings gave the city a Corinthian, Doric and Ionic aspect with colonnades, porticos, domes, frontons and friezes proliferating in all directions. It was a new Rome, decked out in all its finery, though chilled by Irish mists. The collective impression, however, bordered on the austere. Facades were flat and of classic lines, so simple as to be almost banal, built of brick or, preferably, of granite. The only external ornaments were wrought-iron balconies, fanlights over the doors and the doors themselves, lacquered to make them more attractive and sporting brass knockers which were polished every day by the servants. All the richness and sumptuous decor was inside. Stucco and rock-work abounded once across the threshold. The effect was dazzling. Under the influence of Italian licencees the Dubliners mastered the delicate art of plasterwork. Robert West and Michael Stapleton became the most eminent and sought-after exponents of stucco-work. All the ceilings and walls in the capital were adorned with garlands, baskets of fruit, birds, trophies, allegorical figures, *putti*, gods, goddesses and all the paraphernalia of mythology.

The aristocracy – the fashionable people such as Lady Smart and Miss Notable, whom Swift castigated in his *Polite Conversation*, congregated in residential quarters such as Rutland (now Parnell) Square, Mountjoy Square, Henrietta Street, Merrion Square, Ely Place, St Stephen's

55 St Stephen's Green: a triumph of Irish rococo stucco-work.

Green and Fitzwilliam Square. They held court in the prestigious residences of Dublin's halcyon days – in Belvedere House, Charlemont House, Powerscourt House, Northland House, Newman House, Leinster House (which today houses the Dáil and the Seanad, the Republic's two parliamentary chambers), Ely House (which owns a unique staircase on which are depicted the labours of Hercules) and so on. And we must not forget to mention 20 Lower Dominick Street, a little jewel of the rococo. These buildings are today considered to be works of art and some, derelict or turned into offices or warehouses, are in great need of the protection of the Irish Georgian Society (founded by the Honourable Desmond Guinness) and the various defence committees, who fight on their behalf daily against the bulldozers, in an attempt to save and sometimes restore the Georgian heritage.

Some of the architectural gems are less menaced, though their monumental grandeur often makes them appear cold and unattractive. The best example is Trinity College with its impressive Palladian facade. There are also the famous Four Courts and the Custom House, built by James Gandon between the years 1780 and 1790. These two buildings were burnt down in 1921–22 during the war of independence but have since been sensitively restored. And one must not forget the Rotunda Hospital and, in particular, the little Marino Casino, 'the most perfect building in Ireland', an

19

Coming home from fishing along the huge sandy beaches of Dublin bay.

exquisite little Palladian pavilion finished in 1771 and the work of Sir William Chambers.

This was indeed the golden age of Dublin. Not only was there an amazing physical expansion of the city, but it also experienced, in its own small way, a remarkable spiritual revival. It became a brilliant **musical capital** which enlightened Europeans found a joy to visit. Handel conducted the first performance of *The Messiah* here on 13 April 1742 in the packed hall of The Charitable Musical Society. Francesco Geminiani came here on tour. The people of Dublin passionately loved the opera and this was the heyday of the tenor Michael Kelly,

Union and transferred to London. Parliament House was sold off and its premises taken over by the Bank of Ireland. Fashionable society made its exodus to other riparian haunts, notably those of the Thames. On the threshold of the nineteenth century, which produced such great things, Dublin shrivelled in its own misfortunes. For more than a hundred years the city was to see no further development. Decline was inevitable under the prevailing conditions. The only positive reaction to occur was the influx of Catholics into the city. Great numbers kept flowing in from the country districts, driven by misery and famine and so the notorious slum districts were formed. The vacuum created in this way lasted for decades and during this time the capital was without a recognisable identity of its own.

It was to find such an identity as the years went by; that of a crucible of unrest and a catalyst for revolt by the Irish people. First it was the Fenians, then Sinn Fein and the Easter Uprising of 1916, and finally the IRA and civil war. Dublin bore the brunt of the suffering for Irish freedom, in its soul and in its lifeblood. History was written during these savage days when the city became the refuge for patriots, anarchists, revolutionaries, terrorists, martyrs and heroes.

Since that bloody period in its history Dublin has once again changed radically. Now it 'wanders between the sea and the mountains' stretching out further and further, its growth continuing to be fed by the *culchies*, the country people whom long-standing

who was a friend of Mozart.

1800 tolled the knell for this delightfully superficial existence and the city's soaring fortunes plummetted. The independent Protestant parliament was dissolved by the Act of

Sandycove, where the Martello tower once occupied by Joyce was transformed into a museum by Sylvia Beach in 1962: a lecture on *Ulysses*.

St Stephen's Green, given to the city by one of the Guinness family in 1880:
the people of Dublin at a concert.

citizens tend to despise. The larger Dublin has sprawled in all directions, particularly northwards and towards the sea. There are few tall blocks of glass and steel to pierce its sky-line, although the housing problem is as acute here as else-where. Over the past few years, particularly, Dublin has enjoyed an extraordinary boom in demand for new building and hardly a week goes by without some new shop opening in the vicinity of Grafton Street, the high-class shopping area.

Dubliners maintain that their city is easy to live in and marvellously invigorating, offering everything the heart could desire. It is very much alive, being rich in students and theatre-goers, not to mention cinema buffs (and this despite the strict censorship). Each month heralds a new entertainment; the Theatre Festival, the Arts Festival, the Antiques Fair . . . culminating in the traditional **Dublin Horse Show**

in August and the All-Ireland Hurling and All-Ireland Football finals at Croke Park in September.

The past dies slowly here on the Irish coast. As recently as 1966 the Nelson Pillar in O'Connell Street was blown to bits one morning. But Dublin hopes to prove that, despite its depth and significance, the past is, nevertheless, receding for ever. The inhabitants cite their smooth assimilation into the European Economic Community as the perfect example of this. Yet they remain poets and dreamers at heart and they hasten to read – secretly and with delight – those lines of Joyce which describe St Stephen's Green; '. . . the trees were fragrant of rain and the rainsodden earth gave forth its mortal odour, a faint incense rising upward through the mould from many hearts'. They can, at last, get hold of Joyce's works from their libraries – the past is past is a true saying!

Before the
Dublin Horse Show.

2 The Past in the Present

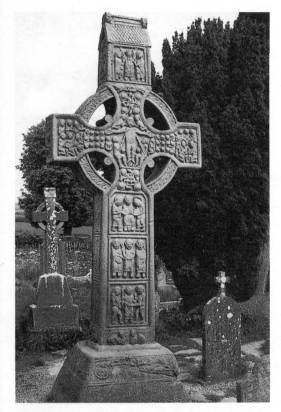

Muiredach's cross at Monasterboice (County Louth), beginning of the tenth century: west face.

These are indeed the last of God's acres, carrying the everlasting stamp of divinity in the shape of humble crosses which date back to the time when the saints walked on this earth. The crosses stand out against the grandeur of the changing skyline, but their roots are in their ancestral peat. The stones are crude, rough and often rough-hewn, now eroded with age and frequently made indecipherable by the passage of time and the weathering of the elements. But here they continue to stand their lonely watch, in a strange timelessness, battered by the driving rain and blasting winds, eaten away by mosses and lichens.

In the pale grey stone dotted with flakes of black mica is carved the symbolic inscription, 'Pray for Muiredach, who raised this cross'. Muiredach McDomhnaill was prior of **Monasterboice** Abbey in Armagh at the very beginning of the tenth century. Monasterboice was then 'an ardently religious city with a hundred crosses', one of those monastic towns that flourished in the Middle Ages and were the crucibles of intellectual and religious life in Christian Ireland. No doubt there were once thousands of crosses like these. Now there are only about 60 in existence, melancholy survivors from what was Ireland's 'golden age'. They come into view haphazardly as though scattered by the Saviour's own hand, often looming like phantoms, when capped in mist or obscured by a curtain of fine rain; or they boldly proclaim themselves against a clear blue sky; or idle in the warmth of one of those wonderful summer twilights with their vibrating colours. The last pearly shades of daylight fall to encircle the feet of Christ on the cross,

flanked by the lance-bearer and the sponge-bearer, frozen for eternity in their memorable gestures. In the dawn the sun reveals **Adam and Eve**, Cain and Abel, David and Goliath, Paul

and St Antony in the desert, then lights up the omnipresent figure of Christ; Christ arrested, Christ crucified, Christ enthroned in majesty, Christ between the saved and the damned, Christ holding the cross and the flowering palm, that triumphant depiction so loved here by the first men of God.

From the sixth to the twelfth century these stone crosses proliferated in

Interior of Dunsany Church (County Meath), stone effigy on the tomb of Christopher, Lord Dunsany, and his wife, Anna FitzGerald, (fifteenth century).

The Anglo-Norman Castle of Trim (County Meath) dating from the twelfth century.

Ireland, replacing the dressed stones of the ancient Celts. Unknown sculptors skilfully carved both the coarse rough granite and the soft grey smooth granite, showing great imagination. At first they used abstract Celtic motifs, then went on to biblical scenes. These as Françoise Henry said, they made into true 'sermons in stone, providing the starting point for a commentary or a theme for meditation', and were used as such by the crowds who daily thronged to the monasteries. The crosses were destined to adorn the monastery courtyards. They were probably painted and were erected so that they faced the rising and setting sun.

Precious relics of the 'Irish miracle', these stone crosses express a rustic fervour. They have the simplicity and naivety of the men of their time, those turbulent warriors who, in the bosoms of their ancient clans, began to turn to Christ as Ireland emerged from a chaotic and myth-ridden past; men who bred a whole string of their own saints, most not recognised by Rome.

It all began with St Patrick the apostle, who landed here in 432. In his wake the pagan Ireland plunged headlong into Christianity with unrivalled enthusiasm and a feverish, unsophisticated splendour. Because it had remained unfettered by the Roman Empire, Ireland had a unique opportunity to remain untouched by the tides of history. On the continent the barbarians invaded and ravaged countries, spreading terror before them. But here in the far west, in this isolated and self-centred country a new world was born. The ancient collective consciousness was interrupted by the creation of an original society whose seeking after the Lord was unrestrained in its passion. The full impact of Christianity which spread from Rome and the East made itself felt here. It struck as a seething, living tide of excessive fertility, into which men fell and became intoxicated with religious fervour. Around this unique Deity an unprecedented spirituality grew up, developing its own language in its Christian art, which showed such depth and such inexhaustible powers of invention. The analogies with jewellery and manuscripts are obvious on these crosses which bear the halos of age. They all show the effect of the ancient and vanished traditions upon the newly-forming civilisation. Christianity only appeared to eclipse the old ways, it could by no means obliterate them; on the contrary, they exerted an even greater significance.

The valley of the Boyne, some 30 miles north of Dublin, is not only the richest agricultural area on the island but also the richest in history, the one naturally giving rise to the other. The highly significant remains dotted about here tell the true story of Ireland's past, though without apparent chronology and with a typical native nonchalance. This is the starting point for a marvellous journey through time, a journey that conjures up the turbulence of long ago, but with pastoral overtones. The capricious landscape of history is sketched out among the green hills and the dark waters of the lazily meandering river.

The first port of call is Slane where St Patrick lit the Pascal fire in 433 as a symbol of the triumph of Christianity. Next is Monasterboice, founded in

500 by St Buithe, a little-known disciple of St Patrick. Then comes Mellifont, the first Cistercian abbey in Ireland, founded in 1142 by St Malachy, a friend of St Bernard, and a handful of monks from Clairvaux (including some master stonemasons of exceptional talent).

After the Christian ruins there is suddenly a great leap backwards in time to prehistoric remains and the mysterious beginnings of society. There is the Brugh Na Boinne of old Celtic legend, an enormous stone-age necropolis, named 'the valley of the kings' by the Irish. The tumuli of Dowth, Knowth and, particularly, **Newgrange**, are the most famous monu-

Newgrange (County Meath): the monolith at the entrance, engraved with triple spirals, about 2500 years before Christ.

priest-kings who are buried in the Brugh. But legend forgets that these High Kings who were revered as symbols of an independent Ireland

Tully House (County Kildare): the Japanese gardens, laid out by Tassa Eida 1906–10.

ments. Here on the tops of the hills, during the third millenium before Christ, megalithic man built these impressive mausoleums (or passage-graves, as they are termed) which are one of the high points in western pre-historic architecture. Newgrange, which shows a certain relationship to the Mycenian *tholoi*, is truly a family burial vault. It is made up of 108 tonnes of stone which have only just begun to be uncovered. It is a huge circular grass-covered mound 90 metres in diameter and 12 metres high. The entrance is gigantic and in olden times was closed off by a pivoting block of stone, behind which runs a narrow underground passage 20 metres long. The walls and roof are made up of great slabs and the passage leads into the very heart of the mound, a funeral chamber enclosing a magnificent corbelled vault six metres high. Everywhere curious decorations are engraved in strict geometrical motifs – spirals, circles, zigzags, helixes, tri-

angles . . . The exact significance of these is unknown. We do not know very much either about those who were buried here with such pomp. Nor do we know who these capable and original neolithic builders were who had the technical prowess to carry out something as delicate as the construction of corbelled vaults. There is little doubt that they came here from Brittany and the Iberian peninsula and were most probably prosperous and peaceful farmers. Carbon-dating has put the date of construction at about 2500 years before Christ. Is this then the true source of Irish civilisation? The answer to this question still lies with those Irish archaeologists who have chosen to study the Brugh Na Boinne and whose research is in full swing.

A few miles to the south rises the hill of Tara, the heart of Celtic Ireland before St Patrick's arrival, and the capital city of the Ard Righ (the High Kings). Legend has it that it is these and whose exploits were sung of by the ancient bards, lived some three thousand years after these communal graves were built. The High Kings, then, have passed on and the pagan divinities are dead, as is the Lia Fail, the stone that roared when the sovereigns were chosen. The mother-hill today is deserted and turned into pasture-land; nothing but a vivid memory embellished by the imagination of generations of story-tellers – those unforgettable *shanachies* – and patriots. The spirit of the place is such, however, that out of the deepest silence

Fox-hunting: an image from the eighteenth century, the almost indelible mark of the British aristocracy.

comes the far-off murmur of royal feasting, homeric revelling, interspersed with song and poetry from which the great national epics were born, martial cycles that bore such a resemblance to the Iliad. Then everything dies down and blurs into the green of the surrounding countryside.

A fine drizzle obscures the view but a secret country can be glimpsed through it, a country of rich pastures full of grazing cattle and thick with quickset hedges and woods. Set amid the hills and shining under the rain are virtually pure Georgian manor houses and castles, symbols of the opulence and dispossession of yesteryear. These well-to-do gentlemen farmers and distinguished landlords are the descendents of that unique race, the Anglo-Irish, who stemmed from the bellicose Norman barons of Henry II, through the Tudor settlers, those small Protestant farmers and landlords, and down through all the other English who had possession of Ireland over seven centuries.

Trim Castle, haunted by its colony of rooks and, according to many people, the most beautiful castle in Ireland, has preserved the enormous square dungeon, the towers, ramparts and barbicans which were the marks of the first 'occupants'. It was built by the Lacy family between the twelfth and thirteenth centuries and was the most formidable of the island's Anglo-Norman fortresses and one of the most important strongholds of the pale, that enclave around Dublin from which the English held sway in Ireland between the twelfth and sixteenth centuries. It was dubbed King John Lackland's castle, after that sovereign's visit in 1210.

The Liffey valley near Blessington (County Dublin).

Carton House in Maynooth (County Kildare): the exterior overlooking the gardens.

But the wheel of fortune was to turn still further. There is a battlefield not far from Drogheda near a ford on the Boyne that today is also a living piece of history. It was here, on 1 July 1690, that 25,000 Catholics under James II, the last of the Stuarts, supported by the French King Louis XIV, joined battle with William of Orange's 36,000 Protestants. The famous Battle of the Boyne was to decide the fate of England, and, in consequence, that of Ireland, for several centuries to come. The Jacobites were routed and popery was defeated. By some alchemy, this battle has become the mythical combat of Good versus Evil for the Orangemen of Ulster who continue to celebrate it in great processions every year, with huge drums punctuating the mass jubilation.

The Anglo-Normans arrived with the blessing of the Pope – the English Hadrian IV. The barons swiftly took possession of the island which proved so profitable to those who stayed on. Towns and markets began to grow up around the fortified castles. All in all it was a felicitous assimilation and the mingling of the races was to be the most painless in Irish history. Traditional culture was, of course, indelibly stamped by it. From Gaelic and Celtic origins, the Irish eventually emerged in their own right and it was then that they began to pose a threat in English eyes, a threat first acknowledged by the Tudors. It was they who began the era of Irish domination; not only having to cope with their 'Irish enemy', but also having to bring to heel the 'English rebels' who had the audacity to claim their freedom from the Crown. The Reformation, then, was to precipitate the most hated form of colonisation, which was in turn to lead to the elimination of the great Irish families and, this time, to the extermination of the ancient Celtic order. This did not occur without rebellion (led in particular by the O'Neill clan),

nor without savage reprisals. Ireland's suffering began in earnest at Drogheda, where the shadows still linger of the siege and massacre by Cromwell's Ironsides in 1649. The Protector declared that this bloodbath was a judgement from God! Deportation, exile, imprisonment and execution became the daily lot of peaceful Ireland'.

Once the Irish had been driven back Westward, Ireland became a settlement for Scottish Presbyterians. Their rule was an iron one with a highly elaborate and cruel judicial and social system. Edmund Burke said that the legal penalties in force at that time were conceived to impoverish and degrade the Irish and to deprive them of their humanity. A period of relative

Castletown House in Celbridge (County Kildare): the Long Gallery decorated in Pompeian style in 1775.

prosperity followed, for those in power, rooted in the vast agricultural lands and the availability of easily hired and fired labour. The eighteenth century was thus the golden age of the Ascendancy, in which the great families built veritable palaces in highly fashionable style on their lands. A few of the grandest are in the most sought-after suburbs around Dublin, such as Carton and Castletown, some 12 miles from the capital.

Carton House in Maynooth (County Kildare) was built between 1739 and 1747 for Robert FitzGerald, the nineteenth Earl of Kildare. The FitzGeralds stand beside the Barrys, Butlers and Burkes as being amongst the oldest Anglo-Norman families in Ireland, and among the most powerful. The Earls of Kildare, later the Dukes of Leinster, were men of substance in the worlds of both Dublin and London. Their huge Georgian residence, the work of the German architect, Richard Castle, is one of the most typical of its genre. The splendid state rooms are decorated in stucco-work attributed to the Francini. They include a beautiful baroque drawing-room in white and gold, furnished with an organ, and a Chinese bed-chamber where Queen Victoria slept in 1849, when she was a guest here with Prince Albert.

Close by, in neighbouring Celbridge, **Castletown House** has the reputation of being the most beautiful Georgian residence in Ireland. The reputation is well-founded, in proof of which the Irish Georgian Society has made it its headquarters – thanks to the Honourable Desmond Guinness, who bought the house in 1965 and leases it to them. It was built in 1722 by the Italian architect Alessandro Galilei, who later designed the facade of St John Lateran, Rome. The fortunate occupier was William Conolly, Mr Conolly of Castletown, the Speaker of the Irish House of Commons: for the Anglo-Irish, in a new attempt to gain independence from London, had now at last got their own parliament and were once again claiming Home Rule. Castletown is the largest of the Georgian mansions and is built in a very severe palladian style. It too houses magnificent rococo stucco-work by the Francini. The Long Gallery with its Pompeian decoration is particularly famous and was executed in 1775 for Lady Louisa Conolly, the Speaker's widow.

County Kildare, with its wide fertile plain, was naturally much sought after by the landlords of former days. It had the attraction of a new rustic and wealthy England, slightly sophisticated yet hardly touched by the Industrial Revolution. The breeding and rearing of horses is a long-standing tradition here and there are still a few of the country's great stud-farms to be found, such as the **Tully** National Stud, where the finest Irish bloodlines are carefully nurtured. Close to Kildare is the Curragh, the most important Irish racecourse. The Irish Sweeps Derby, which is run there every July, is still one of the most important fixtures in the British Racing Calendar.

Castletown House: the main facade with its semi-circular colonnades.

Powerscourt (County Wicklow); the terrace gardens and the Triton Pool. In the background, the Great Sugar Loaf.

Suddenly, further south, the countryside changes entirely. A new world begins only about 12 miles from the heart of Dublin. The first evidence of this is **Powerscourt**, the Wingfield family estate for three and a half centuries, from the time of James I up until 1961. The great house is another of Richard Castle's major works, dating from about 1730. Its aristocratic park was designed in the 1840s and is a masterpiece of great imagination and taste, with its five terraces descending harmoniously towards the Triton Pool and glorious centuries-old trees. All the vegetation shows perfect taste, from the avenues of giant beech trees to the exotically perfumed Japanese garden. Among other features of Powerscourt is the biggest tree in Ireland – a Sitka spruce (*Picea sitchensis*) some 80 metres tall – and the highest waterfall – 120 metres high. The original backdrop of the Great Sugar Loaf, Wicklow's foremost mountain, a tapering cone of quartzite, has been skilfully integrated by the landscape gardener.

Once across this boundary it is the mountain itself that displays a genuine wild and melancholy charm and lyricism. At the gates of the capital are the wide open spaces; the summit, the Lugnaquilla, rising only to 926 metres. The rounded ridges were smoothed down in the last Ice Age, when the inexorably advancing glaciers ground down all the rocks in their path, sculpting the distinctive features of the secret hanging valleys or glens, which are the homes of dark, glistening lakes. There are heathlands here and there, covered in mists and several abandoned peat-bogs. And then there are the forests, mainly coniferous these days and made

Glendalough (County Wicklow): the Round Tower, 33 metres high, one of the best preserved in Ireland.

up of pines, firs and larches which have replaced, here as elsewhere, the great oaks of long ago.

For the lover of the countryside Wicklow is incontestably one of the prettiest districts on the island. It offers him an abridged version, a 'digest', of Ireland's most appealing features. This is O'Toole and O'Byrne clan territory, the ultra-romantic highlands that served so long as a refuge and base for the rebels who were continually sought by the English. There was a brief gold rush here at the end of the eighteenth century, but since then their pastoral serenity has remained undisturbed. The narrow roads that daydream their way across the highlands twist and turn at will, and exude a faint whiff of adventure. They all offer delightful encounters with unspoiled poetry, as well as wonderful views, particularly around the Wicklow Gap or the Sally Gap, or along the Military Road, constructed by the Redcoats in an attempt to stem the guerilla warfare in the mountains. There are few villages, only farms and isolated thatched cottages; and wooded valleys such as the Vale of Avoca, of Clara or of Glenmalure, which are truly beautiful. But it is **Glendalough**, one of Ireland's holy places, that remains the major attraction of the Wicklow Hills. It is tucked away in its lonely valley, the slopes clad thickly with fir trees stretching down to the ruins. The setting is one of pure romance and time seems to have stood still here since the last century. It is not difficult to feel the spirit of the place in this little world hemmed in among its motionless mass of trees and scattered with ancient stones set among wild grasses. Here, more than anywhere else, the ancient mystical Ireland lives again in the extraordinary quality of its silence; the Ireland of those earliest days of Christianity when the ascetics (like the prophets in the desert) made their way through the island on foot, looking for lonely places

suitable for prayer and meditation.

Glendalough was founded in 545 by the anchorite St Kevin, a descendent of one of the Leinster kings. Kevin sought refuge in this valley with its twin lakes – in Gaelic named Gleann da locha – and he made his hermit's dwelling on the shore of the topmost lake, building a simple dry-stone hut nestling against the cliff-face, right in the middle of the forest and at the very heart of the lonely mountains. According to popular tradition, Kevin lived to the age of 120 years. Since he thus had the time to acquire great reknown for his holiness, he was doubtless forced to build a monastery, though this was merely a minute and primitive collection of huts. Eventually even he died. As the years went by pilgrims began to increase; first they came in hundreds, then in thousands. In order to receive them all the monastery had to move to the lower lake in the bottom part of the valley and to grow still larger. And the community did not stop growing. Under the rule of its abbots it became an amazing monastic city, the goal of most important pilgrimages between the seventh and twelfth centuries. At

this significant period for Christianity Glendalough-of-the-multitudes was the western world's answer to Rome. The Annals tell how it was famous throughout the whole of Europe and shone with a glory greater than that of the kings themselves. Glendalough was, in fact, nothing less than one of the foremost 'universities' of mediaeval Europe, disseminating the most intrinsic cultural heritage of the Greek and Roman and Christian civilisations. Drawn by its illustrious reputation, students and scholars flocked to it in droves and batch after batch were moulded there by the great teachers of the western world. It was a veritable hive of learning, full of enthusiasm and dynamism. *Sanctitas et sapientia*, ascetism and erudition went hand in hand. A mystique of writing grew up in its celebrated scriptoria and this cult reached its culmination in the great illuminated manuscripts. Inside its surrounding walls Glendalough bristled with buildings in wood and in stone; simple, unsophisticated edifices in miniature, built to the dimensions of a world just emerging from the mediaeval civilisation. Beside the

Glendalough: the cemetery in the monastic enclosure.

Cottage in Kilmore Quay (County Wexford).

churches stood the abbot's house, the student house, the workshops and the manuscript rooms – the *tech screaptra*. A crowd of strange people jostled one another in the bustling little roadways. This microcosm proved particularly fertile in its combination of austerity and refinement of thought. Indoctrinated in the latinate style, these learned 'pilgrims' soon set out to spread their learning and their faith over the continent, where the great invasions had only recently ceased.

Like others of 'Christ's fortresses' in Ireland, Glendalough was subjected to raids by the Vikings in the ninth century. A succession of sieges, fires, pillages and sackings by these greedy foreigners, who were attracted by the monastery's wealth, left nothing standing apart from the **Round Tower**,

Kilmore Quay, a fishing village.

The Wexford Mummers: a decided taste for the living theatre.

where the community would hastily take refuge during such attacks. The abbot would pull the ladder up behind him - the door was more than three metres above the ground – and there they would cower in terror until it was all over. Then they would go down again and those who had fled would come trickling back. They would cut down trees from the forest and build up once again. Glendalough might well have gone up in flames but it would make a swift recovery, rising once again from the earth, ready to sustain another attack. The extraordinary resilience of this proud city of God was conquered at last, not by the iron and fire of the Viking pirates but by British troops. Glendalough finally breathed its last but the flame of knowledge had already been spread through its exceptional monks whose teachings proliferated.

The appearance in Ireland of these pagan Scandinavians who 'knew neither Pater nor Credo' did not merely result in barbaric fighting and local calamity. They have left a more permanent testimony of their presence in all the island's ports, because it was these heathens who fashioned them, abandoning depredation for this more lucrative activity. In the south of the country at the south-western tip of Ireland, **Wexford** is one of the best illustrations; ford in this context signifies the Nordic fjord. Wexford grew up around 850 in its magnificent site on the Slaney estuary. During the three centuries of Nordic occupation, when the long ships were scattered over the Irish seas, it was a flourishing trading port and a rich town, constructed entirely of wood and surrounded by a defending wall of beaten earth. The locals got on famously with the 'foreigners' here, whether fair or dark, Norwegian or Danish. In 1035 they even converted some of them to Christianity and from then on these seamen and traders also began to build churches. The fate of Wex-

ford was sealed. It prospered under the Anglo-Normans who landed here in May 1169, led by Robert FitzStephen: it continued to prosper under the English. But the great port had its tragic moments too; the first in 1649 when Cromwell arrived fresh from the massacre at Drogheda and gave no quarter to its citizens or to its priests; then in 1798 when Wolfe Tone's rebellion of United Irishmen, led here by Father John Murphy, failed in a welter of blood, hardly surprising since the inexperienced rebels were armed mainly with pitchforks! It was this revolt that led Pitt to put forward the Act of Union passed in 1800. Not until the end of the nineteenth century, however, did Wexford decline as a port, a decline due to the partial silting-up of the estuary, so that the large boats had to use the artificial harbour of Rosslare further south, which is nowadays served by the car ferries of Fishguard, Le Havre and Roscoff.

Today Wexford is a pretty little seaside town with an old-fashioned atmosphere and affords a warm welcome to visitors. You encounter history at every street corner and the delightful older generations of Wexford enjoy the task of relating it. Wexford society daydreams and sings in its lively pubs, drowses a little along its nostalgia-provoking Quay and only really wakes up at the end of October (as it has every year for 25 years) for its delightful Opera Festival, generously subsidised by Guinness, and of a very high artistic standard. Because of it the venue, Wexford's Theatre Royal, has become a meeting-place for music-lovers from the whole of Europe.

The coastline is very beautiful in the surrounding district, despite its undeniable flatness. There are vast deserted beaches with unspoiled sand dunes and lagoons much frequented by all species of waders. The Gulf Stream begins

Great Saltee Island (County Wexford):
a paradise and wonderful nature reserve.

to make itself felt here and this coast is the warmest in the whole of Ireland, with the least rainfall and the most sunshine. It is also the most endowed with fish and the people here make a living through fishing. South of Wexford harbour is the attractive fishing village of **Kilmore Quay**, with its whitewashed thatched cottages, where the inhabitants make a peaceful living catching lobsters and conger-eels.

A little way out to sea from this fortunate coastline rocks can be seen here and there; among them the shining and magical **Saltee Islands**. These deserted islands are untouched in the purity of their ocean setting, veritable treasure islands where it would still be possible to play Robinson Crusoe. Towards the open sea their steep cliffs are fringed with sea-foam. The remainder is covered with a forest of ferns and a carpet of wild flowers. There is no harbour and no humans, only a myriad of tiny rabbits and, especially, seabirds. For here is one of the most important bird sanctuaries in Ireland, indeed in Europe. In the **nesting season**, from the end of spring to the beginning of summer, more than three million birds make these islands their temporary home. Black-backed gulls, herring gulls, kittiwakes, guillemots, cormorants, razor-bills, puffins, fulmar petrels . . . more than 30 species form nesting colonies along the cliff-faces. It is

Great Saltee Island: nesting time
for the gannet colonies.

an unforgettable experience to land on Great Saltee in June. A tremendous strident, raucous clamouring fills the island, composed of shrieks, barkings, mewings, whistlings, groans and cackles. In all directions there are enormous white masses of incessantly beating wings, dancing a fantastic ballet on and on as far as the eye can see. The nesting sites are packed to the roof with no free space at all. Yet by the end of July only a few non-migrant birds or summer residents remain, plovers or sheldrakes, lapwings or oyster-catchers. The rest have gone back to the open sea where they spend the remainder of the year.

But Great Saltee possesses an additional and unique charm: if a man wants to be a king he can be one here, albeit in a modest way. For the fairytale Saltee Islands have their own prince – Prince Charming, naturally! Once upon a time, at the beginning of the century, there was a little boy who, one fine summer's day, visited the island of birds. He was dazzled by what he saw there and made a vow to his mother that one day it should belong to him. And he kept that vow. When he was grown up and had little money, he worked his fingers to the bone until, at last, after many years, he managed to buy his island of dreams. He built himself a limestone throne and was crowned there, in all solemnity, as Prince of Saltee. And thus Prince Michael I entered into Irish history. On this island throne,

A favoured relationship with God over fifteen centuries.

an idyllic, green and beautiful countryside, welcoming under the sunshine. The Irish green, the monarch who reigns supreme here, has woven pastoral delights of an infinite variety and a delicate refinement. Over the centuries 'he' has fashioned a countryside that is now no longer made; one full of peace and restfulness; filled with a sense of quiet well-being and a gentle way of life. Certainly County Wexford is blessed by God. It is often called 'the garden of Ireland' and the appellation is wonderfully suitable, providing you realise that, in Ireland, a garden is mainly composed of grass. Grassy plains, woods, hedges, pretty rivers, all these ingredients combine into an enchanting setting, the freshness and subtlety of which is like no other. At the very heart of this prevailing quietness, a remedy one would think for most ills, whether past or present, history is not entirely forgotten. Mediaeval ruins are dotted here and there in vales and on hills, their walls covered with ivy and peopled by the ubiquitous jackdaws, which are one of the most familiar features in the Irish countryside. The Norman dungeons in particular recall that it was here, around Wexford, during the twelfth century, that the quarrelsome and greedy barons landed, who were to change the island's destiny for all time. It was here they raised their first feudal earthworks which soon changed into those proud castles, the bastions of foreign domination; here, too, where the first settlements grew into towns around the defences. Such is **Thomastown** on the Kilkenny road, an ancient Norman fief which today is a mere shadow of its former self.

In the wake of the Anglo-Normans came the Cistercians, whose splendid ruined abbeys are scattered throughout the area; Tintern, Dunbrody and, particularly, **Jerpoint**, the famous daughter-house of Mellifont, founded in 1180 on a pastoral site in the Nore

which stands in the open air, he had engraved the message that this was a symbol for all children, showing them that with hard work and perseverance they too could realise their dreams. There is a message for adults too, a maxim that encapsulates his little country saying that no man is truly free unless he prizes freedom above all things. The Prince of Saltee, a Dublin gentleman, is now an old man, but he still spends part of the year on his island in the modest little house he keeps there. And the fairy tale goes on because the succession to this inestimable crown is assured by Michael I's heirs!

On the mainland the grand dreams of the open sea quickly give way to more simple earthly pleasures. Here is valley. The spirit of the place has been preserved, as has the austere poetry of its stones, where the Gothic and Roman styles harmonize perfectly. But the most amazing features, and principal attraction, are the cloister sculptures, added in the less rigid fifteenth century. These knights and saints can say more about the depths of Irish originality than numerous learned dissertations.

After the faceless white-robed Cistercian monks, the centuries and men have played tricks with the geography round this area once again. In the neighbouring Barrow valley, in particular, was felt another, more contemporary, force which was all too soon to vanish. Not far from New Ross is the hamlet of Dunganstown, lost in its surrounding greenery. It was here that in 1820 Patrick, the great-grandfather of President John Fitzgerald Kennedy, was born. The ancestral farm has been pulled down and a more recent one stands in its place, where distant cousins still live. The President came here in 1963 when he visited Ireland and resolved to trace his trans-Atlantic origins. The Kennedy cult was

The ruins of Jerpoint Abbey (County Kilkenny) where the spirit of the Cistercian monks lingers.

an elegant testimony of the Renaissance. The town has a long history behind it, closely linked to that of the powerful Butler family, the Earls of Ormonde, who owned and ruled over most of the south. Apart from its enormous English-looking castle, founded by Strongbow, the town is mainly famous today for its Beer Festival which recreates, under an Irish heaven, the joyful and amazing carnival atmosphere of the Munich Beer Festival. The Kilkenny Festival takes place each year in May, lasts a week and has the reputation of being one of the most unruly popular events in the country! Of better repute are Kilkenny's Design Workshops, established by the Irish government to promote a high standard of industrial design. These workshops and studios are housed in the sumptuous eighteenth century castle stables and most of the decorative arts are represented, from basket-making to goldsmithing, from glass-blowing to weaving,

Waterford glassware: a secular art known throughout the world.

extraordinarily active in Ireland from the time of his election. While he lived, almost every Irish home displayed his photograph, placed piously beside pictures of figurines of Christ and the Virgin. On his death, the murdered President continued to be honoured as a national hero – the symbol of individual success that always haunts the Irishman's dreams. A little way out of Dunganstown, on Slieve Coillte Hill, is the very beautiful Memorial Park, endowed by Irish Americans, (ever-mindful of their origins) in recognition of their mother-country. These emigrants are held up as shining examples of success by the sons of Erin, even though the latter no longer leave Ireland for 'the promised land'. The Memorial Park was inaugurated in 1968 in a solemn ceremony performed by Eamon de Valera. It is a vast and tastefully laid-out aboretum, covering some 200 hectares and containing more than 6000 species from the five continents. But these trees and shrubs will not reach maturity for a quarter of a century yet, and so one's impression remains of a strange forest in miniature. It will grow taller as memories grow smaller and remembrance fades.

Kilkenny is not far away now. Kilkenny, city of rich merchants, containing Rothe House, the only Tudor house in Ireland that has survived the rigours of time to remain

Kilkenny weaver: the rebirth of an historic craft.

from pottery to the graphic arts. They have achieved notable success both at home and abroad in only a few years, so justifying their existence and underlining the fact that when good taste and talent combine, as they do here, quality and beauty are inevitably the results.

One jump further south and here is **Waterford**, another of history's great meeting-places and another port at the end of a fjord. Its fate, too, has been strangely identical to that of Wexford, except that there they remained loyal to the British crown though opposed to the Reformation. The local speciality is crystal glass, which has found its way around the world since the end of the eighteenth century when the English colonials took it with them on their travels, at the height of the Empire. And Waterford glass still enjoys a

Thomastown (County Kilkenny). The huge shadow of a not-too-distant past.

world-wide reputation today. Just here, on the banks of the River Suir, is the invisible frontier dividing Leinster from Munster – two different worlds, particularly in the past. One side of the dividing line looks toward Dublin, the other towards Cork; one side revealing country farms and manor houses, the other nothing but desolate mountain ranges, apparently endless moorland, wild and jagged coastlines. But even though the harpist's lament is no longer heard rising from the deep-set dwellings, the past still shows itself here as a recurring and fearful fate.

3 The Far South

20,000 years ago neither horses nor greyhounds existed in Ireland – come to that, neither did the Irish! The Emerald Isle was completely white, buried under ice and frozen snow. In this inclement wasteland of the last Ice Age, hardy species of Arctic animals evolved. Polar bears bathed in the waters of the River Suir, reindeer and elk wandered across the Tipperary tundras. Then, gradually, the glaciers began to melt and recede northwards, whence they had come. Dense hardy grass started to grow; forests reappeared and eventually covered the whole of the land. Soon there was nothing but green in its infinite variety of chlorophyll. It was then, around 7000 or 6000 years before Christ, that man – the Mesolithic hunter and fisherman – arrived in the north-east of the country, in Ulster. He came from the south-west of Scotland, apparently having crossed the narrow arm of the sea in leathern coracles. Until about 3000 years before Christ few would-be immigrants were really attracted to this island which was so far to the west. Then the Neolithic agricultural society grew up, where man began to live in denser communities along with domestic animals. These farmers colonised just about all the fertile lands on the river banks and around the lakes. Eventually, probably during the fifth or sixth century before our era, the Celts emerged with their warring tribes and horsedrawn battle chariots. It was in truth with them that the horse and the dog also appeared, in the form of the stocky pony and the primitive mastiff, who were to become the ancestors of the Irish horses and dogs. And it was then, too, that Irish horsemanship was born, that undefinable concept of a perfect relationship between the man and his horse, born out of knowledge, sympathy and love. If such a skill is, as some claim, 'in the very marrow of their bones', then its origins are far back in the past when the Irishman became the horse's most noble conquest!

A few details are useful here. Mediaeval Ireland already had its racing horses, the hobbies, as well as its hunting dogs, elegant animals that were subsequently named hounds to differentiate them from the common dogs. The **Irish Wolfhound** is the foremost of these, a swift and agile giant of a dog who, during the Roman times, was sent to Rome to take part in Circus games; during the eleventh century the great King Brian Boru raised packs of them for his hunting parties. From the Renaissance onwards, under the English influence, the native breed of Celtic pony was crossed with the supposedly more noble horses from Spain and the East. This resulted in the cream of horseflesh, known today throughout the world – the thoroughbreds and the hunters (and even the Irish draught horses, those

Irish wolfhounds: they hunted wolves up until the eighteenth century.

'Harriers' — they trail hares from November to March.

gallant beasts of burden that work in the fields); horses that Ireland has exported for centuries and which still represents one of its main occupations.

This long-standing and exceptional tradition of horse and dog breeding is carried on with enthusiasm often bordering on passion, and explains why race courses and greyhound racing-tracks are national institutions. It also explains why the racecourses are not merely frequented by high society, but also are the favourite places of entertainment for a whole population. Why, too, hunting – particularly fox-hunting and **hare-coursing** – are sports esteemed in equal measure by all rungs of society's ladder. It is a fact that this is a country where horse and greyhound racing take place virtually every day. The extreme popularity of these races also, of course, reflects the gambling instinct which is a very prominent feature in the Irish character – you have only to see the impressive number of thriving betting offices which cover the country and are full of customers, year in and year out, to appreciate its strength!

Horses and greyhounds are omnipresent here and completely integrated into daily life – there is even a sort of fusion between the animals and the countryside itself. They are seen literally everywhere, particularly in the gentle, soothing country of **Tipperary**, where several of the country's stud farms are situated and

County Tipperary: a land where the horse is king.

Cashel (County Tipperary): the ruins of the rock;
the Round Tower, the cathedral and the
archbishop's palace (tenth–twelfth century).

where Clonmel, the home of the Irish Coursing Club, is one of the principal venues for greyhound racing. The rich plain of Tipperary, closely ringed by mountains, is one of the favourite places for Irish breeders, from the very small farmer to the large stud proprietor. The majestic horse here, like everywhere else in Ireland, has an individuality, a typically native personality, characterised by independence, willingness, calmness, balance and sociability – like the humans who surround it! The best school here (for horses and for humans) is the hunt itself; the winter chase when they have to gallop for hours after the fox, across an amazingly varied terrain, where banks, ditches, hedges, brakes, streams and dry-stone walls succeed one another without respite and at a pace that fills both horse and rider with an indescribable intoxication. Everything is done according to a well-tried and tested ritual. And so it is hardly surprising that steeplechasing is the island's speciality. But just imagine that there was once a time, under the terrible Penal Laws, when no Catholic in the country was allowed to own a horse worth more than £5!

Right in the middle of the plain dedicated to equestrianism, under the mare's-tail clouds, rises a mass of stone, looking for all the world like a becalmed ship of strong rib and sturdy back. This is the romantic **Cashel**, standing firmly within its closed walls, the fortified capital of the Munster kings; a strange ruined

Ardmore: the west face of the 'cathedral', decorated with blind arcades and romanesque sculptures.

Cashel: the last traces of the great capital of the kings of Munster, in the desecrated athedral.

'acropolis', standing alone, seemingly on the edge of time itself, fixed in its rustic setting, the sole remains of vanished dreams and grandeur, which are unceasingly recreated both in the silence and in the howling winds. The only splash of colour, apart from the green of the surrounding countryside, is the soft greyness of the rock with its strange tones of light purple, a scene in half-tint, evocative of past splendours.

Between the fourth and twelfth centuries one dynasty became predominant in the south, here on the Rock of Cashel, in the same way as that on the hill of Tara in the north. Saint Patrick came here expressly to convert King Aengus to Christianity and it was here that he first used the shamrock as a means of explaining the Holy Trinity to the friendly and curious pagans. Once the Druids had been convinced and the Celtic gods Christianised, then History (with a capital H) could begin in earnest; and this it did, with great promise. In 977 Brian Boru was crowned king on the Rock. In 1101 the kings offered Cashel to the all-powerful Church and the bishop-princes hastened to embellish the site. Their particular genius is evident in the Cormac Chapel, consecrated in 1134, which today is considered one of the most important achievements of mediaeval Irish art. It is truly a masterpiece of ultra-elaborate architecture, exceptional in Ireland, with its stone roof showing such mastery of technique, its light bas-relief tympana, its fluted capitals, transverse ribs, diagonal ribs and arches adorned with highly original sculptured heads; a workmanship almost baroque in its execution, that smacks of the archaic. It is without doubt 'one of the most astonishing anthologies of Romanesque art imaginable'. The chapel, then, is a testimony of a golden age; the jewel of a religious capital; a mystical product of a new kind. But, sadly, the rich and influential Cashel was to be swamped in the tide of history. In 1171 Henry II came there to receive homage from the Gaelic chieftains and the whole of the Irish clergy. After that the rock once spat upon by the Devil, as the legend goes, had to struggle to keep itself alive. It was subsequently sacked and burned and finally abandoned in the middle of the Enlightenment. Today Cashel is one of the best-known and most visited spots in Ireland; scarcely little more than a poignantly melancholy scene, exuding an imperceptible sense of silence, rest and nothingness, swelling across the meadows into infinity.

On the horizon, in all directions, stretch gentle, blue-tinged mountains; the Galtees with the wonderful Glen of Aherlow and the beautiful Mitchelstown Caves behind them; the Slievenamuck and Knockmealdown ranges, not long ago inhabited by eagles and wolves; the Comeragh and Monavullagh mountains . . . plains, forests, lakes, then, suddenly, a little way off the meandering tracks, are luscious valleys thick with rhododendrons and murmuring with freshwater salmon rivers – the number one being the Black-

Cork, the greatest Atlantic port in Ireland.

water (not to be missed by the amateur fisherman!). In these valleys nestle simple little villages, very peaceful and untroubled spots such as Ballymacartry, Ballyporeen, Clogheen, Cappoquin. Time passes by here in a uniquely unrestrained and inimitably natural fashion – that wonderful Irish time, the ultimate Heaven-sent blessing. Even frenetic continental travellers have to slow their pace here unless they want to risk a nervous breakdown! There are few clocks and scarcely any watches in this relatively undeveloped island; only the slow pulsation of the days. One generation passes on the secret of marking time to the next. The Irish certainly know instinctively how to deal with time, just as they know how to treat horses – they are undoubtedly the last westerners to have such knowledge.

The way leads almost imperceptibly down to the coast. Half-way between Dungarvan and Youghal is **Ardmore** on its picturesque cliff-side setting, priding itself on the possession of the most beautiful round tower in the country, four stories and 30 metres high. A monastery was founded there by St Declan in the fifth century and, in the middle of a charming wooded cemetery, there are still some remains of an elegant twelfth century cathedral whose western facade of blind arcading is decorated with really remarkable Romanesque sculptures. Adam and Eve, Solomon, the Magi and St Michael the Archangel all share the somewhat limited space in perfect harmony.

Then comes Youghal (pronounced 'Yawl'), linked with Sir Walter Raleigh, who was given enormous estates here by Elizabeth I, who wished to 'plant' English colonists in the area; he also lived here at the end of the sixteenth century. After Youghal is the main road to Cork, though a detour must be made by way of Cóbh. Cóbh (pronounced Cove) is the main harbour for ocean-going ships arriving

A sea-fisherman, from fifteen years old.

in and leaving from Cork. It has its letters patent of nobility as far as the nautical world is concerned in that it boasts the world's oldest yacht club, the Royal Cork, founded in 1720. Cóbh has long been a port of call for the great liners and has specialised in transatlantic crossings. It was from here in 1838 that the *Sirius*, the first steamer to cross the ocean, started her voyage. Much sadder memories are evoked, too, since it was from here that many thousands of emigrants sailed, particularly during the last century after the Great Famine; crammed in frightful conditions on board the notorious coffin ships, though full of hope that, should God spare their lives, they would be welcomed in the United States. And the last view they would have had of their native land would have been these sad, grey quays, packed to bursting point with desperate, yet fortunate suppliants – fortunate in that they were still alive.

Cork is the second capital city of Ireland and the Republic's highly important Atlantic seaport. Set on the hilltops at the bottom of the Lee estuary, Cork is a large city, traditionally devoted to commerce and industry. Its rise to importance is a

classic one – a Celtic monastery first (founded by St Finbarr); a Viking base; an Anglo-Norman market town, where an important Gaelic community congregated under the aegis of the powerful MacCarthy clan; a flourishing English city – in fact, outwardly, in its architecture and urbanism, Cork is perhaps the most 'English' of all the other Irish cities. It was subject to all these influences, yet has lost none of its intrinsic individuality. Conquering powers were soon absorbed and alle-

end of a hunger-strike lasting 75 days. He wrote, 'It is not those who persecute the most, but those who suffer the most, who will be the victors.'

The days of anger are over. Now the dignified and stately capital of Munster is a lively, active place, particularly around its historic heart, clasped between the two arms of the Lee. St Patrick's Street, Grand Parade and South Mall, the main roads, are full of banks and shops, swarming ant-hills full of victims of the newly ram-

Baltimore (County Cork), where land and sea are one.

giance was only superficial. Throughout the trials of the centuries, the people of Cork remained unalterably pure products of Erin itself. They were hardened rebels when they had to be, in adversity, and very courageous in battle. They refused English rule on three historic occasions: in the sixteenth century at the Reformation; at the end of the nineteenth century during the Fenian revolt; at the beginning of the twentieth century with the 1916 uprising and the 'troubles' of the 1920s. The notorious IRA brigades (particularly the Third) are widely remembered here for their harrassing of the Black and Tans. Cork, then, was one of the most tenacious bastions of national resistance, symbolised in the self-sacrifice of its lord mayor, Terence MacSwiney (writer, poet and ardent republican) who died in 1920 at the

One of many pubs.

pant consumer society. Industry thrives: steel, petrochemicals, shipbuilding, cars (Ford built one of its first European factories here), textiles and (of course) beer and whiskey. All these have arrived to shake the people out of their traditional nonchalant attitudes, to galvanise their energies and revolutionise their thinking. Cork has chosen the modern dream. It wants to be an 'in' place and is almost

Cork: quays along the River Lee.

aggressively avant-garde – partly perhaps due to its natural aversion to Dublin! There is a very active cultural life of great artistic freedom, in the theatre, ballet, music and painting. It has deliberately become part of an international circle – hence the Film Festival, which shook off the rigid censorship a long time ago, is of a very high standard. And this city which, they say, has given Ireland its journa-

lists, teachers and civil servants, today has produced three of its best writers – Sean O'Faolain, Frank O'Connor and Daniel Corkery.

Some have condemned Cork, with its decidedly urban appearance, as ugly, sinister and gloomy. But the ubiquitous presence of water in the shape of canals, **quays** and bridges give it a certain charm, reminiscent of Holland, according to some, or of

The traditional gypsy caravans, dear to the tourist office.

The joys of riding, not far from Kinsale (County Cork).

all chiselled out with headlands, coves, deep and jagged indentations. A tiny coast road, still relatively unused, though one of the most attractive in Ireland, runs from Cork to Bantry. The interior of the county does not lack features of beauty and interest: towards Mallow or Macroom or, in particular, Lake Gouganebarra, set in a splendid forest (national parkland since 1966) at the foot of the Shehy mountains. History flourishes there, too, in its violent form, from the Munster White Boys (the early rebels who terrorised the countryside in the eighteenth and nineteenth centuries by daring to attack the all-powerful landlords), to the IRA members of the 1920s, who based their guerrilla activities in the lonely, mountainous hinterland of Cork. Nevertheless, it is the seaboard here that exerts an unflagging fascination; that strange, vast expanse along the far Atlantic coastline of Ireland. **Kinsale** is the first charming spot to visit, an historic port of exquisite refined obsolescence. Here, lurking fleetingly in the dusk, are the plumed and bearded phantoms of the old hidalgos from the Golden Age; Spanish allies, the religious fathers who, during the bloody seventeenth century rushed to help the last of the Gaelic rebels with a Don Quixote-like army. In a more restful era Kinsale

Venice according to others; a somewhat exaggerated description, since there are none of the architectural refinements that give such subtlety to those beautiful aquatic cities. In fact the real charm of Cork lies in its everyday life: in the pubs, where sportsmen and punters (and, goodness knows, there are enough of those!) gather at all hours and where the lilting local accent is a source of wonder, always whetted by a devastating humour – 'the little worm of derision that gnaws at the soul of Ireland'; and again in the labyrinth of tiny old streets climb-

ing up to the hilltops; or in the street stalls of the Cornmarket towards the Coal Quay; or again in the motley bric-a-brac of the Antique Market. Or, quite simply, in the incessant comings and goings of the boats in the dynamic, humming vitality of the port which looks out across the water.

At the end of Cork Harbour, just beyond Crosshaven, is the open sea. As well as being the largest county in Ireland, Cork also has one of the greatest seaboards, with mile upon mile of rocky coastline, beautiful enough even to eclipse that of Brittany,

54

Bantry House (County Cork): an Italian garden on the Irish Riviera.

became a very popular haven of peace. Today fishing – it is one of the most important sea-fishing centres (particularly for the blue shark) – and sailing are its main money-makers. All the yachtsmen who come over have a soft spot for this gentle, friendly port with its picturesque old pubs, always bursting at the seams, and not only with locals!

The further south one goes along the chain of pleasant rias, habitats of an impressive bird life, the wilder the countryside becomes, with no vestige of domesticity and the more imposing the limited features become. Timoleague, Clonakilty, Rosscarbery and Glandore are mere fishing villages, but have an irresistible fascination with their old stone and carpets of flowers. The coast is festooned with blood-red fuschias and small golden beaches of fine sand loll lazily in the sunshine. This is countryside purified and miraculously preserved from ecological damage, without proliferating urbanisation or pollution, with an untouched wild life; in fact, in its original, virginal state.

Beyond Skibbereen, on the south-

A Kerry countryside: here the great solitary spaces of the west begin.

The cruelty of the land, and of the sea . . .

ernmost fringe of Ireland, the sea and the mountains are even more closely united. The sea is everywhere, dotted with a rosary of islands and islets, popular with conservationists; an azure sea, often sparkling and a shade too blue for these latitudes, trimmed with a hem of white breakers that come in to smash themselves on the deserted beaches, amid a silence that evokes the end of the earth, just like a film in slow-motion. There is a last glance at history in **Baltimore**, the town that supposedly lent its name to the

The renowned Killarney lakes.

Dingle, the peninsula with the greatest expanse of ocean.

Dingle, a Gaelic mini-capital.

Mass on the small island of Skellig Michael.

American city. At the beginning of the seventeenth century this small fishing port was attacked by Barbary pirates and a large proportion of its inhabitants found themselves in Algeria as slaves.

Now, released from the rough demands of time, you may take a deep dive into the heart of the elements, into magnificent nature with a thousand secret nooks and crannies. Out to sea from Baltimore, is Cape Clear Island, the first enclave of the *Gaeltacht*, where a famous seabird observatory was established in 1959. Further out is Fastnet Rock, nostalgically recalled by yesterday's Blue Ribbon winners. Not far away to the west are the formidable sandstone cliffs of Mizen Head in the extreme south of the country.

Through each of a thousand twists in the thickly wooded road, the view slowly builds into a crescendo of natural splendour. But the land itself is rough, uncultivated and terribly barren. Everywhere there are signs of exodus and abandonment, houses that are now nothing but wind-swept shells, half-tumbledown dry-stone walls, patches of earth as large as pocket-handkerchiefs. It is a land of mourning, despite the southern sunshine, depopulated during the last century by the Great Famine. Between 1845 and 1850 the Angel of Death passed this way: thousands died – beside a sea rich in fish, but the people had no tradition of fishing so they grew only potatoes – thousands emigrated. But in direct defiance of death, the peasantry was not entirely driven out, though they cling today to mere bits of wall and a few acres of sheep-grazing land. The mountains have gradually reclaimed their own. The people who kept their traditions alive for so long have little hope for the future.

The air has become warmer and balmier. It is even hot, according to Irish standards. The rain gods have given up and gone away in discouragement. Now bathed in light, **Bantry Bay**, with a kind of blue radiance, bites deeply inland. For the first and last time there is an enormous blot on this harmony of water – the price of the effort to survive – the large local nuisance of the petroleum terminal of Whiddy Island, constructed right in the bay by the Gulf Oil Corporation in 1969, where supertankers come to discharge their crude to a disturbing sound of pumping.

The three large, uneven-sized and jagged peninsulas in the southwest – Beara, Iveragh and Dingle – are considered to be among the jewels of Ireland, the regions of old Celtic magic, stretching out as they do, like long fingers into the open sea. The best-known of the three, the Iveragh peninsula, contains the famous Ring of Kerry and the tourist-ridden Killarney; the western peninsula, the Dingle, is the richest in archaeological remains; the eastern, the Beara peninsula, is the wildest. When it comes to beauty, the rough, characteristic beauty of high, unspoiled lands, Beara and Dingle are almost equal

Beara of the legendary mists is a world apart, of a spell-

binding wildness and crazy romanticism. First there are the Caha Mountains, their slopes rising slowly and rhythmically upwards to form a backbone on the ocean between Bantry Bay and the River Kenmare, marking the natural frontier between County Cork and County Kerry. They are bare and deserted, an austere mass of nothingness; really little more than mere undulations (Hungry Hill rises only to 675 metres), rounded hillocks like grass-covered waves breaking here and there on a rugged chaos of rocks. But along the mountain ridge, where the subtle changes of light and shade waver continuously, the real and the imaginary are constantly blended – as though the spells are working at a zenith of perfection. And so one reaches Kilmakillogue Harbour, one of the most enchanted spots in Ireland, to one's eye recalling the charm of a Japanese water-colour, particularly in the dawn or dusk light. Fraying streams of mist issue from the coves across the surface of a motionless sea having the texture of watered silk. An opalescent sheen plays on the water reflecting the incessantly massing or dispersing clouds. Phantasmagorical trees melt into their sleeping shrouds of mist on the river banks. It is a weird, apparently timeless, country, continually distilling an inescapable dreamlike essence. The luminous mass of foreground, background and distance is diffused by successive refractions into a slow drifting that splits mysteriously into a secret, intangible and ostensibly sacred universe where the imperceptible ravages of time can nonetheless be glimpsed. Real architecture reveals itself in lyrical, baroque and mobile forms, like a film set for a forgotten retreat of a legendary and immensely beautiful Celtic princess. An indistinct, fairy setting, broken by flashes of sunlight: a doorway opening into the mysterious. Everything seems to come together and then blur, becoming immaterial and, thus, an

illusion. Then, all at once, towards the mountain peaks, from where the irradiating light dissolves the mist, there are both harsh and gentle changes; gashes as clear as crystal, tenuous unveilings, where the hidden powers that move this world can be glimpsed, albeit momentarily. In a climate of total unreality, one's journey suddenly

The Gallerus Oratory: an architectural masterpiece of the first Christians.

becomes an inward one, a poetic wandering in osmosis with the weave of the land and following the same threads.

As is the tradition with all magic spells, the absurd extravagance of the natural surroundings is unexpectedly, almost sensually, stupefying. The exotic abundance, the sensuous emanations, take even the most blasé of visitors by surprise. Here, incontestably, the 'tropics' are unexpectedly revealed as a remarkable gift of God and, especially, of the all-powerful Gulf Stream. Ireland is certainly generous both in its uncommon riches, and in its contrasts! The 'Riviera' is not the least of the surprises that she holds in reserve. For here is a luxuriance that

seems to conceal some trace of a very gentle lifestyle. Here are the sumptuous Italian gardens of Garinish Island, where George Bernard Shaw came to write *Saint Joan* in the twenties. Here is the amazing park at Derreen House, with its thick shady jungle which one must admit is completely unusual in these latitudes. Palm trees, eucalyptus and aloes, and a multitude of succulents suddenly spring to view along the trout streams, amid the wonderfully romantic peat-bogs. And there are tall ferns, giant rhododendrons, azaleas by the thousand, splendid conifers, yew-trees, sorbs and, as always, the ubiquitous fuchsia.

On a more banal note, the main town of this enchanting realm (whose dense vegetation is its true trump card) is Glengarriff. Year after year, in its own careless fashion, it attracts thousands of tourists away from the Mediterranean or the Caribbean. Relaxation is the rule here, aided by the azure sky and a pervading air of calm – even the grey Atlantic seals sprawl out in the sunshine in total peace. This is far

An annual task: renewing the thatch.

from being the case in its rival, Killarney, revered by flocks of tourists. This is another botanical and subtropical high spot some 20 miles into the interior beyond Kenmare. This town is the Mecca for the country's tourists, one of the absolute 'musts' of an Irish holiday – at least according to the travel agents! It has become a principal focus of organised tours, which swallow up the miles in standardised comfort. Killarney has many hotels built especially for tourists, typical open-air evenings and countless souvenir shops. Here everything takes second place to tourism – the town bears the indelible stamp of it. One can criticise but basically the phenomenon 'works' wonderfully and is not without interest. One has only to look around to ask oneself whether all of Ireland will not eventually experience it; thought-provoking, for the Irish as well as others?

Though Killarney has experienced the irresistible rise to being a tourist metropolis, in the surrounding area the countryside remains beautiful in spite of all, even if its beauty has been sullied by being exploited as prime material for this avalanche of holidaymakers to discover. And the town itself has been heavily affected. Its new look is brash and, one must say, somewhat ugly. The former 'pearl' of Kerry has become, unfortunately, something of a conveyor-belt to speed the tourist on his spending way throughout the holiday season. To entertain the visitors there are 'traditional' horse-drawn carriages, which have been designed specially for sight-seeing in the countryside, catering for the most varied range of customers, offering luxury, budget and economy

class! It may have been considered 'the thing' for the gentry of past centuries to come here, to hunt the deer or to rhapsodise over the 'terrifying' spectacles of its waterfalls and lakes, but today, regrettably, Killarney would attract few such people and is no longer frequented by poets and painters. It is one of the very rare spots in Ireland where the tourist 'industry' is in such evidence. Thankfully the three famous **Killarney lakes** have not been ravished by the crowds. With their lush green semi-islets and their clumps of bamboo and magnolia, they remain, out of season, the 'jewels' so boasted of in former days, enshrined in large, thick woods where the red deer (today no longer hunted) gambol in peace. And the surrounding area, magnificent in its fertility and much prized by dedicated fishermen and hunters, preserves its irresistible attractions almost completely intact. It literally overflows with riches, each one as delectable as the last: Muckross, the first national park to be created in Ireland; Inisfallen Island; Dinis Island; Lough Guitane and the Mangerton Mountains; up to the universally known Gap of Dunloe, that amazing glacial furrow, a narrow passage between green rocks set with tiny lakes, where hundreds come to serve their rough apprenticeship on the local ponies (which, for some reason, guides persist in calling lethargic!). Here nothing is easier than to shake off the heavy trappings of the hardened tour organisers. Stress quickly disappears because there is no lack of open space. You have only to put on your own seven-league boots – for which read walking boots, pony or bicycle – to find

Rich colour
enlivens
the scenery.

At the most extreme tip of Ireland: fishing villages on the Dingle peninsula.

Farmers and landsmen as well as sailors.

yourself speedily in the mountains at the heart of the country's highest range, MacGillycuddy's Reeks. As a preliminary, you must understand the terminology because the pinnacle of the Emerald Isle, Carrantuohill, scarcely rises 1040 metres in height, which is undeniably small. But the wild grandeur of its old worn summit, which has undergone all sorts of experiences, gives it an undeniable charm. For the enthusiast it even offers short steep climbs which are, apparently, nothing like a rest cure. In any case its solitude and exhilarating freshness have a calming influence on the unceasing summer hordes and sometimes in the wintertime there is snow. . . .

The ever-popular Ring of Kerry is certainly worth the detour. From Parknasilla to Glenbeigh the coastline is superb and the beaches enormous. Worth seeing are the impressive Staigue Fort, the pretty Lough Currane and, especially, the Skellig Rocks a few miles out at sea. Little Skellig is a fantastic reserve for gannets, like Great Skelling or **Skellig Michael**, where a small community of anchorites lived between the sky and the sea in the age of saints during the sixth, seventh and eighth centuries. These anchorites must have long enjoyed reciting that famous poem by St. Columba that goes, 'What joy it is to be on an island, on the crest of a rock, and to watch the ever-changing face of the ocean and to let the eye follow the long glinting waves which sing the praises of their Creator in their ceaseless course.' There is Valentia Island, too, the departure point for the first transatlantic cable; Caherciveen which some say is closer to New York than Dublin is; Killorglin with its notorious **Puck Fair** in August, a homeric cattle fair where, in immemorial pagan tradition, a billy-goat is crowned king while stout and whiskey flow in rivers.

The most beautiful is yet to come – the wonderful **Dingle peninsula** that stretches out here at the westernmost tip of the western world towards the far Americas. It is a haven of a very singular peacefulness, far away from all uproars, an endless dotted line of lost glens running the length of the Slieve Mish mountains for some 30 miles as far as Slea Head. It is a complete and distant world, a primitive, infertile and hard world, which began through fishing and the building of *currachs*, those rough prehistoric boats that are still used by the men of Dingle. It stretches towards Dunquin, Smerwick, Ballyferriter and Ballydavid towards the foot of the mountain named for St Brendan – the saint who may have discovered America, who wrote one of the 'best-sellers' of the Middle Ages and actually came here in retreat before setting out on his great voyage. It is a world that has not yet been seized by the tentacles of modernity, rich as it is in Gaelic heritage and the last traces of a dying civilisation that ought not to be totally lost. Those responsible for the Kerry *Gaeltacht* (a Gaelic speaking area) have not been lacking in imagination. Against the prevailing tide of forward-looking

A mediaeval banquet at Bunratty Castle (County Clare), an essentially American activity.

fashion, they have conceived the original Gaelic Summer Schools in which, for the space of a summer, the unsophisticated natives of the region act as language teachers for a youth in search of its roots. So traditions continue, but at the very end of this long and thin peninsula there is a pathetic and mournful symbol – the Blasket Islands. These ghost-islands have now slipped their moorings, I think, and are bound for the open sea, abandoned by their last inhabitants in 1953 at the end of two thousand years of over-harsh living. At the least breath of an offshore wind they will set sail for good and be swallowed up into the ocean.

The route passes through Georgian Tralee, the capital of Kerry, with its infinite sandy beaches, and climbs up to Limerick – another capital of another county – County Clare – and considered a very 'smart' place in the last century. Within range of Shannon Airport, **Bunratty Castle** gives an old-fashioned and stylish welcome ('mediaeval' banquets and the like) to new arrivals from across the Atlantic, forming in great numbers to sample the rich variety of their ancestral lands. The Burren is not far from Bunratty and forms, with its formidable Moher cliffs, the most captivating natural curiosity in this area, preceding the transition to a softer countryside. The Burren is a desert – technically a karst or rough limestone country; a beautiful stone desert strangely clad with an unusual Alpine finery – gentians, saxifrages and orchids grow there at will, unusual in these latitudes. Countless megaliths are scattered in these rocky solitudes. A new world begins here: the gates open flush into the west.

The Poulnabrone dolmen, right in the middle
of the Burren (County Clare).

4 The Irish Lakeland

The Irish equivalent of the Mississippi is called the Shannon; the longest (222 miles) and the most beautiful river on the island; the most majestic, too, stretching out in perpetuity to the heart of vast open spaces that one would say had been flattened by God's own hand. Its source is in County Cavan, 49 metres high in the Shannon Pot on the lower slopes of Tiltinbane in the north of the Iron Mountains. From there it flows in carefree meanders from lake to lake, from north to south, neatly cutting Ireland into two, both geographically and politically. On the left bank is the east, historic and submissive Leinster; on the right, the west, wild and rebellious Connacht. As it makes its way to the sea, the Shannon irrigates the large central plain – the widely stretching Midlands (judiciously renamed Lakeland) – but, it must be admitted, it drains the area very badly. Beside its dark and lazily flowing waters the countryside changes abruptly during its slow course. Waving plains of grass and gently rolling green hills give way to marshland and peat-bogs. Extraordinarily flat, empty, monotonous countryside unfolds, often with an air of sadness, where everything is swallowed up into the vastness of the sky as the clouds seem to rise unceasingly from the melancholy depths of the drenched earth. The countryside is waterlogged and fluid; the strange tones of mauve and brown continually dissolve and blur into the shivering veils of mist. The countryside seems endless, scattered with numberless lakes – or rather loughs – enshrined in this 'grassy ocean'. The Shannon flows through a good many of these, the largest being Lough Ree and **Lough Derg**, which behave like small internal seas with blustering winds and dreadful storms. Finally, once past Limerick, at the end of an Amazon-like estuary – difficult to decide what is ocean and what is river in this 60 or so kilometres of viscous, sea-green, wind-torn water – the Shannon dies away between Kerry Head and Loop Head, as it meets the white-crested Atlantic.

Today between the Shannon's source and its mouth there is an eloquent contrast which says much about the 'economic miracle' of the seventies. Round the upper waters there is a spectacular pocket of poverty, a deserted country area, virtually lifeless: County Cavan and County Leitrim have long been classed among those most strongly affected by emigration. In the lower reaches is a profitable industrial complex, a clear symbol of Eire's recent prosperity: around Shannon's international airport a new town has mushroomed as a result of the dynamic industrial policies followed by the young Republic. Attracted both by financial and fiscal advantages – this is a virtual free zone – and by the

Men honouring St Ciaran at Clonmacnoise.

A Romanesque masterpiece: the Clonfert portal.

cheap labour, firms from America, England, Japan, Holland and Germany have erected ultra-modern factories, swiftly followed by much less attractive constructions. Here, between Europe and America, two steps from the 'Old Man River' dear to every Irishman's heart, transistors and high class pianos, synthetic diamonds and luxury textiles are turned out, as well as the most sophisticated electronic equipment. All around crowd brand new houses, bristling with television aerials. For once, it does not matter if the charm of the traditional environment has been lost – at least nowadays the local younger generations will not need to join the throng of exiles!

For those going up river in small holiday craft **Killaloe** is the departure point; Carrick-on-Shannon the finishing point. The flotillas of cabin-cruisers, of which the tourist industry is so proud, have to contend with slow, dark waters. The river has created its own world here. Apart from a few discreetly-placed power stations, telling their beads of turbines and kilowatts in homage to the god Electricity, the countryside is untouched for the length of the Shannon, a large motionless corridor, harmoniously ordered and flecked with lonely ruins, as romantic as any heart could desire. Inis Cealtra, the Holy Island, the castles on Lough Derg . . . apparitions from another age follow one upon another on the ghost-ridden river banks, where bards and funeral watchers loom unexpectedly from the misty mazes on the surface of the water. Time and centuries melt into one another as the water flows on in millenial rhythms. Rediscovered is the eternal, archetypal Ireland and its litany of saints, monasteries and high carved crosses . . . St Brendan the Navigator (who 'took the cloth in order to be humiliated and live like an exile in worldly life'), he who laboured from Antarctica to the Antilles, passed by **Clonfert** in 563. There is nothing left of the community he founded. Only

The Shannon near Portumna at the end of Lough Derg (County Galway).

the cathedral's superb **Romanesque portal**, dating from the 1160s, bears witness to the subsequent importance of this rich and influential seat of the church. Truly this portal of carved heads, showing a rare artistic virtuosity and 'an entrancing extravagance', is an exceptional piece of highly sophisticated architecture – 'a great blaze of creative imagination' as Françoise Henry described it. There are both traditional and imported elements: again an extraordinary synthesis, a wonderful symbiosis between the old Celtic universe and the new Christian and Latin thinking, nourished with a strong continental flavour, reminiscent of Saintonge and Poitou in particular. It is an unexpected portal for the monks, with six recessed orders, all richly embellished with carving, reflecting a cunning play of light and shade to the arches with their relief and perforated decoration . . . 'all crowned with the unique triangular pediment, its cornice of small pillars and blind arcades and its over-ornate triangles and heads'. Such a profusion of carved heads, like so many unanswered questions, set against the moving sky, belonging as much to heaven as to earth.

The waterway contains much that is unexpected. Soon, to starboard, there is **Clonmacnoise**, on a patch of rising ground dominating a bend on the river. Its two round watch towers are ash-grey against the green that stretches as far as the eye can see. Here is the centre and heart of Ireland and one of its most important cultural centres. A home of the spirit, fixed here on the bank of the river that laps against a fringe of grey shingle, left by an ancient glacier in the middle of this swampy land; here where long ago the primitive forest flourished and where the brown peat has reclaimed its rights. The setting is original in the extreme.

The dead Clonmacnoise is now prostrated with ancient sorrows, eaten

Flowers for eternity.

Clonmacnoise in its mantle of silence. (County Offaly.)

up with inexpressible sadness, but once was the exemplar for the whole of western civilisation. It was one of the original matrices, one of those very first monastic cities which, for a few brief centuries, were thronged with students and intellectuals – the great Alcuin himself, Charlemagne's illustrious tutor, came here from Aix-la-Chapelle where he ran the palace school. Clonmacnoise, then, knew the way to excel in teaching and in transmitting a living culture. Legions of copyists and chroniclers toiled within its walls. Sculptors and goldsmiths with their original creations used materials in an entirely new way, proposing different interpretations of this universe inhabited by a unique God. Like the Ancients before them, the new generations of thinkers began an amazing collective dream. The

royal and princely families of Erin bestowed their patronage and watched over this glorious 'fortress of Christ' with a vigilant concern.

Today nothing exists of this radiant past and its magnificence, except memories and, in the cemetery, an unexciting archaeological site, a scanty grassy area, set with eight miniature churches and two splendid crosses, carved in 900 and 1000. These are more than just modest remains; these ruined churches exposed to the four winds summarise some thousand years of prayer and history – an intense, harsh and violent history, and one too soon faded. This staggering monument of one of the most fruitful communities was founded by St Ciaran, the son of a chariot-maker,

Imperceptibly the setting changes with the passage of time. Athlone, the capital of the Midlands is also the most important town on the river, with its swans, floating hotels and jolly hurly-burly of river traffic. It is a pleasing city, full of genuine liveliness. Further on, just to the north, spreads the great sheet of water that is named Lough Ree, very famous for its 23 islands and, especially, for its eels. Here the true fisherman's paradise begins – in a country where the fisherman reigns supreme. There he is, in fantastic numbers, in raincoat, cap and boots, armed with rods, lines, hooks, bait and landing-nets, congregating from all corners of the earth. Doubtless St Peter recruited his most ardent followers here! This famous 'lake district' has

Towards Lough Ennell (Westmeath): setting off to go fishing.

about 545; brilliantly developed by its abbots; survived the usual vicissitudes, buildings fired and razed and monks slaughtered like sheep. Between 834 and 1012 Clonmacnoise was pillaged 18 times and burned 26 times by the Viking warriors who sailed the river – Turgesius, the fearful pagan chieftain, even committed the ultimate sacrilege by allowing his wife to recite oracles from the altars. After that it was attacked and ravaged dozens of times by the petty kings and chieftains of the Irish clans themselves, in search of plunder. It finished up being sacked and reduced to nothing by the English garrison from Athlone, under the last Tudors. This was the final blow: since then a mantle of silence has fallen across this desolate enclosure – a silence that today is broken only by the chugging of pleasure boats below, and by a few open-air masses.

Where the pike takes cover in the surroundings of Mullingar.

Swans on the Shannon: a species much in evidence.

certainly features to attract even the most demanding in the counties of Roscommon, Longford and West Meath. Fish are to be found in great profusion:
salmon, trout, pike, perch, tench, bream and others of the carp family . . . you
have only to make your cast and the subsequent struggle will certainly be raised
to an epic level. Just consider, in proof, the multitudes of stuffed fish that adorn
the smallest recesses of the district's idyllic inns (though judging from their size,
there must have been a miracle at some stage once they had left the water!).

The avenue of water has narrowed now. The Shannon is splitting, deviating,
tacking between the first green undulating hills. The **swans** are still travelling
on it, so are plovers and woodcock. In terms of game and fish this country is
abundant. At the heart of this magic land of water is **Mullingar**, one of the
greatest fishing towns with its myriad of lakes – **Loughs Ennell**, Owel, Derra-
varagh, Sheelin or Gowna . . . belonging exclusively to the silent race of fishermen
in their reedy haven of peace – what Heaven must have been for the first Christians!

The river's charms are by no means exhausted. The sailors of this gentle water
are well aware of the fact, for they have many a time watched the flight of herons
in the softening light of dusk. In countryside that looks like that on canvases
painted by Constable they have moored by pretty little villages with crammed
pubs where all the local farmers like to spend their evenings – and so even do
their regal-looking wives. Besides they have seen the procession of phantom
villages and abandoned hamlets, the unreal remains of the very first years of the
nineteenth century – the high point here for water transport and river navigation.
Linked to Dublin and the Irish Sea by the Grand Canal and the Royal Canal,
the Shannon was then a much frequented route, teeming with water-coaches and
sailing-barges. But,
sadly, the arrival of
the railway, followed
by the disastrous
Great Famine,
brought the gracious
era of water-transport
forever to a close in
Ireland. Traffic
stopped all at once
on the river and it
was not until the last
decade that the
Shannon came to life
again, with the aid
of water-based
tourism, born out of
English investment.
But its new life is
truly magnificent
and has an incor-
rigible air of
romance about it.

Mariners of the still waters . . . or the prodigious 'boom' in pleasure boating.

The River Shannon not far from Killaloe (County Clare). Only the paddle-wheels are missing.

5 The Western Lands

Man of Aran, that admirable film made by Robert Flaherty, lives on in the memory of all who saw it. This drama of the sea, the fight for life by peasant-fishermen at the ends of the earth, has subsequently been raised to the heights of myth, though the heroes, the last survivors of the Gaelic civilisation, hardly claimed to do more than keep body and soul together. The beautiful and harsh pictures of life in the raw on this austere archipelago meant that this poetic film had a tremendous impact from the moment it was released. Under the astonished eyes of the Europeans of the 1930s, a new, primitive and forgotten world 'was born', a world of absolute purity and austerity. They were amazed at the discovery that on their contracted planet, a stone's throw away from the feverish megapolises, this strange parallel universe still existed, in a timeless state as far removed from their own as that of the furthest galaxy. It was a shock to the consciousness of the man in the street who had been unaware of its existence. It must have heralded the beginning of a search that has not yet finished, taxing the sensibility of our so-called modern age.

But the Aran Islands had already been 'rediscovered' – since the first years of the nineteenth century when scientists had begun to study this Atlantic microcosm because of the interest of its antiquities, its flora and its indigenous population. This was particularly true in the very last years of the century when John Millington Synge went there several times (on the recommendation of Yeats) in search of inspiration and an authentic national lifestyle. This famous dramatist even made it the setting for his great work, *Riders to the Sea*. Aran had given him living material for the message he wished to put across, as from the heart of the Gaelic revival. And so the biblical simplicity and the beauty of this archaic community, so miraculously preserved, had come to light at this period in history. Synge wrote that the lives of the people here have the strange quality that is found in legends and in the most ancient poetry, after he had summed up the countryside in the concise phrase, 'I have never seen anything so desolate'. There was no clock on the islands then and fairies and evil spirits still haunted the heathlands. After God and his priests, the *shanachie* was king, weaving dreams and superstitions into everyday life. And when one of the islanders died, 'keening' was still the custom – that extraordinary funereal lamentation howled by the women during death vigils and burials. The chanting would rise, a slow, wild, earsplitting sound; would break off and silence would momentarily reign; then rise

Men of Aran: they cling with an unequalled tenacity to the culture of their ancestors, those great Gaels of Ireland.

The stone fief and its miles of low walls.

part, be it for good, or bad. It first appeared in the sixties and has made relatively great strides since. The Aran Islands have become a 'must' for tourists in Ireland. Inishmore, the largest of the three, and the furthest west, is still the only one to have been touched by this busy and lucrative holiday season. The other two islands have neither harbour, nor jetty, and *currachs* have to be used to help ferry visitors across – at the moment this limits the invasion. Young people in particular, eager to get back to nature, have appropriated this ancient and reputedly 'virgin' land. But the islands' magic could almost be played out. The search for the picturesque is fast making it vanish and the quest for the unusual will do the rest. And that is even without considering what these oceanic islands have to offer by way

up again, louder, cutting through the crying and the howling of the wind – a sorrowful age-old lamenting, a pagan despair.

Inishmore, Inishmaan, Inisheer . . . three bare, arid, wind-swept islands, but a single retreat for men and history, facing a pitiless ocean. Cut off from the rest of the world and shut in upon itself for a long time, this enclosed community had bred its own race of men, made its own laws and lived its own life for centuries, having slipped all moorings with the outside. The guide books call it the 'conservatory of ancient Ireland'. But the three islands are not at all what they used to be. There were 3000 living on them at the turn of the century when Synge was there; today there are 1200. On the other hand, they are endowed with electricity, television and even the aeroplane! And lifeless modern brick-built houses have replaced the thatched cottages of yesteryear; modern innovation always works by making existing things unattractive! Would modernity then be the slow death for this handful of islanders, as it has been for so many others? Apparently not. Depopulation was acute at the beginning of the century but it seems to have been arrested: emigration is not now considered as the only future prospect, even though relatives in America continue to send money home to those still remaining: unemployment seems to have been eliminated. It is an exceptional fact here that the young people stay on the islands because they wish to. Small work-shops have been started to help them do so and jobs have been deliberately created. Fishing has been considerably developed and trawlers bought. The hard, good life of Aran is one possible choice today for those who insist on remaining on their ancestral lands and poverty is not such a crushing burden to them, as it was to their parents and grandparents, mainly thanks to state subsidies. Thanks too, to an innovation which has gone a fair way to bring about this revolution; here. as elsewhere, summer tourism plays an important

of beautiful white sandy beaches and a relatively warm water temperature. Hotel resources are still very modest – it is still customary to stay with the local people – and this limits the annual intake today. But housing sites have recently gone up in value quite considerably. So tomorrow, perhaps, a second Mykonos could mushroom here. It is a real danger, despite the Aran people's wisdom in deciding just to wait and see.

The steamers which have brought people and mail from Galway for decades are full to bursting-point. The boutiques selling **Aran knitwear** (those famous chunky-knit white sweaters that all the island women make) have flourished in the streets of the cosmopolitan 'capital' Kilronan. These traditional handcrafts are already in world-wide demand

Dún Aengus: the most impressive pagan fortress, dating from the Iron Age.

Aran knitwear: work carried on at home and proving rather lucrative nowadays.

At Inishmore, totally 'home-made' land.

dence of the very first Irish dry-stone architecture – oratories, chapels, primitive churches; such is Teampall Bheanain, one of the finest in Ireland and a real jewel, overlooking Killeany Bay. These remains date from far-off times, when the islands, then the illustrious 'islands of the Saints' were the home of great faith and learning – St Enda founded a well-known monastic school here in the fifth century. Then the Aran Islands shone like the westernmost lighthouse of the known world.

On the fringe of an Ireland itself on the fringe of Europe . . . these **men of Aran** already belong to another world, exposed to the madness of the winds on their poor pebbly fields. Face to face with the elements, with adversity, with extreme misery, they are living proof of a fantastic tenacity. But will they resist their new future, now exposed to new winds, those of the economic and social integration that threatens to destroy their traditional culture? There is certainly no question of their renouncing their ancient

and the islands no longer have enough sheep of their own to meet it, so wool must now be imported.

After each boat docks a great crowd throngs the main road from Inishmore: processions of rented bicycles, caval-cades of horse-drawn carts. Everyone must see **Dún Aengus**, the huge prehistoric stone fort on the cliff top 100 metres above the Atlantic with its triple ramparts and fearsome *chevaux de frise*. According to scholars, this is the most mag-nificent barbaric monument in Europe; and undoubtedly the work of daring builders. One should not forget – and the holiday hordes take care not to – that the Aran Islands have several of these Iron Age forts, which are the most remarkable of their kind: Dún Eoghla, Dún Eoghanachta, Dún Duchathair, Dún Chonchiur, Dún Formna . . . as well as many dolmens and cairns. They also have significant remains from the beginnings of Christianity, moving evi-

. . . a line of countless generations of stubborn peasant-fishermen.

The men set off with the currach.
The women begin their wait . . .

customs, even though the keen has almost disappeared – albeit only recently. One has only to attend an island mass in Gaelic to be convinced of this. First of all the language persists; that is fundamental, and the beauty of their voices sublimates it to a poetic intensity. The guttural Celtic tongue, with its amazingly flexible and soft inflections, does wonderful things to these songs of everlasting hope that come from the depths of time. And the national dress still exists, being worn particularly on a Sunday: long black dresses and huge embroidered black shawls for the women and for the

home. There are lots of children to help, for big families still survive, come what may. These simple, mysterious people of Aran appear invulnerable. They are tall, roughly-made people, often with Herculean strength. If you believe the legends, they would be direct descendents of the notorious Firbolgs, the first Celtic settlers in Ireland. But, in fact, a little English blood got mixed in somewhere along the way, probably during the seventeenth century, when Cromwell posted a garrison on the islands. Whatever the case, they are different genetically, physically and psychologically from the other inhabitants of the west of Ireland. And their longevity, no doubt due to the excellence of the air, has long been the subject of admiration: centenarians are often to be met with; 120 is an accredited age; and they even talk about 150!

Only about 60 family names remain. Dirrane, Conneely, Flaherty, Hernon . . . regular brothers who have shared the squalls, the drizzle, the long winter storms, the fog in which some of their number have been lost at sea, and the brilliant azure summers. But above all

these are men with foam and salt in their blood, familiar with the strongest of seas. They are built for the rough hauling necessary to sail their dark *currachs*, those light little boats made out of skin stretched over a wooden framework, a design going back to antiquity; and for working the land, that is their only treasure, that land acquired only through incredible effort. There is little soil on these islands, which actually form part of the old rocky reef linking the coast of County Clare to that of Connemara, being a geological extension of the neighbouring lifeless and barren Burren. The soil, then, has been created by the islanders themselves over the generations. They actually 'made' it. They began by preparing the future fields, stretches of petrified grey limestone, strewn with huge blocks of granite; these stones they made into miles of low walls, patiently and precisely marking out the land to come, acre by acre. Then they broke it down, pulverised it with sledge-hammers, progressively levelling the surface. And then they fashioned the soil itself: a bed of living sand, duly selected from

men, woollen jackets and grey woollen trousers and coloured belts known as *criosa*: all homespun, of course, and woven at home. And, for everyday wear, they still have *pampooties*, those hard-wearing rawhide sandals, which have to be soaked in water to stop them drying out; these too are made at

A tankard of stout, one of life's pleasures.

A universally renowned Connemara pony.

The ubiquitous obsession with horses . . .

In Joyce Country, the incredible harvest.

Lough Corrib or the solitary man's paradise.

the beaches and spread with a layer of seaweed; then a second layer of sand, mixed with the sparse native clay. Then they waited for several seasons. At last sowing was possible and the artificial soil proved fertile. Potatoes, rye, other vegetables and cereals and grass for the animals grew in the little walled enclosures. With the addition of fish they now had the means of surviving in their closed economy for centuries.

They have not allowed old customs to die out on Aran. They still build *currachs* and continue to make their own soil. Less men are lost at sea these days than they were in the past, but the work is still hard, as monotonous as the breaking surf. Life's rare pleasures are, as always, the simple ones – the pub, stout, sing-songs, joyful reels and jigs danced on festive occasions and conversation with its limitless resources. Watching-out for bad weather is an inborn trait. Their souls are strong, but so is the complexity of what threatens to defeat them. And perhaps it is really only a matter of a stay of execution for the men of Aran, deep-rooted and stubborn as they are; perhaps the 'temptation' of the mainland will finally carry them off, sooner or later. The mainland is so close; it can be seen clearly on a fine day as a misty blue backcloth, a long lateral stretch of land to the north – the undulating line of the Twelve Pins or Bens in the heart of Connemara. It is from Connemara that the indispensible peat has come for centuries. From here, too, came the horse, which the men ride bareback to the clattering of hooves. It is one of the most familiar sounds on the Aran roads – that and the braying of donkeys. The Aran horses are none other than those gallant and universally known **Connemara ponies**, one of the most original of Irish breeds. They live here in almost complete freedom, as do their masters, and frisk gaily across hills and glens all the year round – except sometimes in August when their owners round them up at Clifden for the famous and colourful Connemara Pony Show, which is a ceremony dedicated to this hardy little horse, attracting breeders and enthusiasts from all over the world.

This alluring mainland also contains the shining, well-to-do Galway, with its totally bourgeois respectability. It rises in gentle tiers from its silted-up bay, snuggly huddled around its gloomy port with its screaming gulls overhead. Galway is not particularly picturesque or appealing. Despite this, the west's sombre capital, with its keen interest in economic survival, does not appear melancholy but leads a rather happy life in an indefinably unconcerned way. It is a little urban hydra, no doubt stimulated by the sea air, and displaying a dynamism which is rather unusual hereabouts. It is a recent transformation, though, because its historical fame, in which it likes to bask – that of being a flourishing commercial centre in the Middle Ages and the Renaissance, with strong links with Spain and France – is no longer valid today. Cut off in mid-flight in the middle of the seventeenth century, savagely sacked and burned by Cromwell's troops as a reprisal for having dared to support a Catholic king, the rich city of ship-owners and merchants, bristling with gold and galleons, never recovered. It has come back to life today, unobtrusively re-constituted in the Common Market era, because (appearances apart) it has moved with the times and because the National Tourist Board, the Bord Faílte Eireann, has made it a turn-table at the gates of the romantic deserts of the west. Its dreams of long ago had to be put aside. First and foremost it had to forge ahead by imitating developments coming from the east as closely as possible. Bands of adventurous tourists stop off here nowadays on the trail of the· great summer migrations, visitors of every race, but particularly Americans and Germans, following the clearly defined lines laid down for them ; the onslaught to the west starts here now – the

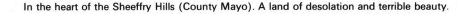

In the heart of the Sheeffry Hills (County Mayo). A land of desolation and terrible beauty.

itinerary says so!

Connemara is the beginning of everything. No one would deny that the nine letters of its name spell magic; magic evident in its wild and unusually beautiful open spaces, talked of in all the books. Areas exerting such magnetism and retaining such poetry are

Kylemore Castle, built by a Liverpool millionaire at the end of the nineteenth century. Today it is a Benedictine convent.

rare in Europe. Every journey here virtually has to be a sentimental one, be it in a small, large or passionate way. It is a country that goes right to the heartstrings immediately, answering even the most stringent demands of the imagination – an unparalleled and rare showcase. There is nothing like it for making one fiercely 'Irish' and this is, naturally, of great value to the Bord Faílte. People come from all over the place to seek that dream without which the human spirit withers and dies, even in an advanced and liberal society. It is a truly engaging land which at one and the same time both offers and conceals the smallest of its secrets; a land of prodigious beauty and purity, mysteriously im-

passive, where space and time suddenly seem to expand at leisure.

The ritual declamations are made of clichés. It may sound hackneyed but all the attractive elements are here – the peacefully rolling emerald mountains, the archipelago of lakes, the rushing mountain streams where the salmon leaps, the darkly interwoven **peat-bogs**, the light-purple heathlands, the blood-red fuchsias in profusion, the white-washed thatched cottages lost upon the moors, the incessantly smoking peat fires . . . These images can be reproduced *ad nauseam* for the nostalgic imagination, but form too a matchless solitude where escape is finally within one's grasp. There is nothing superfluous in the setting. It is a simple kingdom of stone, of granite in the south, of shale and quartzite in the north; not forgetting the famous green marble that is highly prized by so many and which provides a profitable export. The scene is enclosed only by the old worn-down mountains, which already smack of the salt sea, the stocky fortresses of the Twelve Pins and the Maamturk in County Galway, and the Mweelrea, **Sheeffry** and Partry in County Mayo.

Achill Island (County Mayo).
'If the fire goes out, the house will fall down,' as the saying goes.

The finely-chiselled coastline is considered one of the most splendid and lyrical, replete in its enjoyment of the sea with thousands of scraps of islands, long beaches of fine sand or coral, deep bays, sharp promontories and endless fjords. Truly Connemara provides a wonderful tonic and it is impossible not to succumb to its magnetism. It is an unequalled feast that should be devoured very slowly by way of its winding roads, secret pathways and boreens. The rambles here, whether along the coast or on the mountains, are well worthwhile in their healing solitude. One can cover mile after mile in this strange desert without meeting a living soul. It is unbelievable that the crowds converging upon Connemara

can somehow become dispersed and disappear like magic. Only a deep, shattering, almost inorganic silence reigns. Right in the middle of the roads are strange, unobtrusive figures that quickly become familiar on closer examination – small wild horses with blonde or silver rumps, docile black-headed sheep, donkeys, cows, sea-birds ... virtually everything that you could meet with on an Irish road in the way of wandering animals, without which the west would not be the same. And lastly, hovering over it all is something intangible – a feeling of the essence of Ireland, an authentic aura, that original aura which wells up on a level with the mist in this subtle anachronistic land, illuminated, as Nerval would say, by 'the dark sun of melancholy'.

One thing certainly makes itself felt. In this privileged, idyllic and unvaryingly beautiful Connemara it rains a good deal. To tell the truth, it rains assiduously and in enormous amounts. Rain can fall unceasingly here for weeks, even months – as witnessed by that memorable year 1923 when it rained 310 days out of 365 around Ballynahinch; a record even for rainy Ireland! And grumblers grumble about the lack of sunshine and warmth, without realising that this disastrous weather is, perhaps, a Heaven-sent blessing, because it helps to protect Connemara from the scourge of our times and keeps it unspoiled. Without a doubt if the pouring rain were not here the area would rapidly fall prey to multitudes of international holiday-makers, who now in small numbers plough around it in raincoats. It would become one of the most frequented spots, disfigured and degraded. Thank goodness, then, that fate has seen fit to impose its saving climate! For the numerous connoisseurs their happiness is made complete by the vision of a suitable half-tone of this last-surviving land of dreams caught up in the grey-

The Mulrany beaches
along Clew Bay
(County Mayo).

Peat turf, the national fuel.

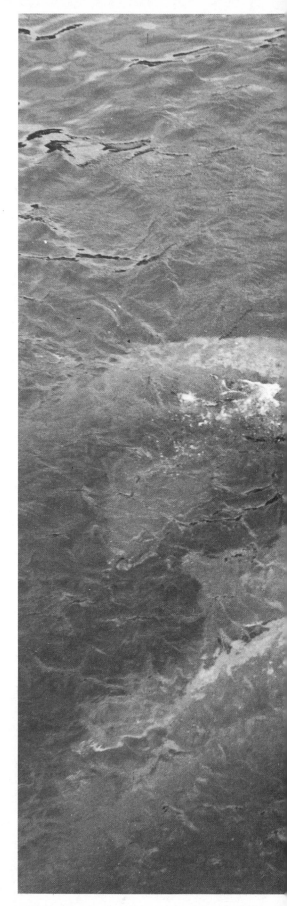

ish, indistinct mist, appearing from time to time from behind its veil of oblivion, when the highest peaks cannot emerge from the heavy livid clouds, when the rain sheets down and drenches the land, a far cry from the insipid and dull chromolithographs.

Yes, everything is beautiful in this stronghold of inclement weather, even the rain. And everything is unexpected. The huge **Lough Corrib**, dotted with tiny wooded islets. The **Joyce Country** around Cong, that John Ford used as the mythical country for *The Quiet Man*. Roundstone and Errisberg, and the breathtaking views from up there – on a day when it is not raining! The rough, tempest-torn Renvyle peninsula with its great Atlantic swells. Killary Harbour, a veritable Norwegian fjord, whose calm waters stretch out over almost 12 miles. A jump northwards discovers the serene splendours of Mayo. The incredible **Clew Bay**, which should be seen at low tide, and its throng of islands, dominated by the majestic pyramid of **Croagh Patrick**, the holiest of all the holy mountains in Ireland and in July the impressive setting for one of the country's most fantastic pilgrimages in honour of the

Apostle who brought Christianity to the Emerald Isle and who chased away the snakes (literally and figuratively). Still further north, past the aristocratic Westport, is **Achill Island**, a true miracle of solitude among the seals and the blue sharks – the latter are still fished for in the traditional manner from single currachs. Further and still further up is Belmullet and its mysterious bays where wrecks of ships from the invincible Armada sleep on, destroyed and conquered by the will of the ocean.

So much beauty can go to your head, so be careful because the cocktail that awaits you here in the poetic west is even stronger than the notorious poteen, the secret brew that has made its inhabitants drunk for centuries. For this is a tragic beauty. The natural beauty may be harsh, violent and jagged in itself, but it masks a scarcely completed cycle of horror. For a long, long time it has walked closely with death, throughout three long centuries of history with tragedies that still cling to this wretched land, crushed under the weight of its sorrows. The string of miseries is indelibly stamped on it; the black anguish of famine, exile, exodus,

Fishing for the blue shark off Achill Island.

And the unemployed, those perpetual exiles, are still forced to leave the country to stay alive, though now they emigrate to England.

When Cromwell came to Connacht he renamed it hell. Before his time, the

Those who have survived . . .

depopulation, unemployment and, as a finale, slow death. These were immense catastrophes that shattered whole generations; terrible bloodbaths that drained the west of its vital energy. For those who lived through it all, hanging on to their mountains whatever the cost, the extreme poverty of yesterday still exists under an apparent improvement due mainly to tourism. The wretchedness of the west has not long passed, the period of absolute penury when everyone was poor, in rags and starving, living a pitiful existence in shabby little smoke-filled cottages that squatted at the foot of the glens. Only 15 or so years ago, from Connemara to Donegal, it was not uncommon to meet barefooted children on the way to some far-distant school. Thankfully, this is no longer seen today. Even the mysterious tinkers, those outcasts of fortune, those gypsy tin-repairers who wander ceaselessly up and down the island following their well-beaten trails, have abandoned their old wobbly horse-drawn caravans for mass-produced, motor-drawn vans. A sign of the times! There is no longer the atrocious destitution of the past, only underdevelopment in the industrial age. Of course, there is no pollution, but there is an inveterate archaism, a deep-seated immobility.

Norman and Welsh barons had already driven back the independent Gaels into the west beyond the Shannon. These grasping barons – who were to become the ancestors of the notorious 13 tribes of Galway – were perpetually fighting with the Irish clans (particularly that of the O'Flaherties) for possession of the land. Never-ceasing squabbles were followed by rough melées between warlike bands who were always spoiling for a fight. But

and their irreplaceable helpers.

Lough Gill (County Sligo), dear to the heart of the poet William Butler Yeats.

the west had as yet experienced nothing worse than brutal customs and a harsh existence. It was only when the fanatical Cromwell compared Connacht to hell and chased the native Irish there (with the help of his terrifying Ironsides) that the country literally became so. Hell became the lot of those Roman Catholics who would not submit and they became the living damned. Driven from the rich eastern lands by the English colonists, the wretched papists soon flowed into the furthest corners of their divided country. The ultimate irony is that, by a quirk of history, these 'absolute deserts' of the west which today constitute a breathtaking emptiness, suffered from overpopulation for three centuries. They were peopled by dispossessed 'savages' and serfs, who retained nothing but their own tongue and their own saints. They were considered to be 'drunken, lazy and dirty and reduced to the state of beasts' by the plundering landlords and soon came to epitomise absolute despair. Amid the violence and the nameless hatreds, the west became the last enclave for the incessantly persecuted Gaelic families, but they could not hold it. There were peasant revolts and rebellions, followed by bloody reprisals. At first, during the hated Penal Laws, there were illicit 'hedgerow schools' where inheritors of the rich ancestral culture attempted to impart it to the children. And stealthy open-air masses were held, always drawing an impressive crowd of the faithful. The silent, secret, west became the stronghold for Celtic and Catholic life, cradled in clandestine illegality. Then there were the dreadful ravages of the Great Famine during the Industrial Revolution that scarcely reached this far west. Hell was now embellished with a crushing apocalypse for its people, still remembered today. The horrifying potato blight, the dying who wandered the roads, cholera and other contagious epidemics, hunger gnawing at the entrails, bodies piling up in great mounds and millions of dead filling up the cemeteries. And finally departure, for the hardiest, without any hope of return, in the 'floating coffins' that sailed for the promised land on the other side of an ocean . . .

The west then was reduced to this: crowds of peasants driven from their lands through hunger and, soon, by the great absentee landlords and their systematic evictions which increased between 1860 and 1870. The tenants were unable to pay their rents and so their small-holdings were beleaguered and their barricades smashed open by troops. There were thousands more emigrants as a result and the west literally emptied. The only ones who remained were those who could do nothing else, apart from the indomitable, the rebels and the outlaws from other provinces, whose numbers were growing and who took refuge in the mountains and islands of Galway, Mayo, Sligo and Donegal. The tradition of resistance against the occupying power is a long and unceasing one, full of audacious attacks, desperate combats and murder. It embraces the IRA of the twenties, during the troubles, when they had their bastions and training camps in this land so suited to guerrilla activity – and they continue to have secret bases there. Throughout the cycles of history the war has been unceasing, embedded in the heart of the Gaelic community.

Has the west now done with the past and really exorcised its ghosts? The divisions that lacerate it are still visible. The great catastrophes have left behind them a land deprived of its lifeblood, peopled largely by old men and, today, children. The fracture seems irreparable. The west of Ireland is well used to dying or mastering death and it remains a land still steeped in the anguish of a segregated society. Even though the despair and vehemence of ancient times is over, the bitterness remains in people's souls. A strange

Somewhere in Sligo,
the eternally blooming rhododendrons.

numbness is present everywhere, a kind of quiet desperation, a sharp sorrow at simply living, without taking account of the memories. The west has dwelt so long upon its past dramas and sorrows that it has ended up by taking refuge in words and conversation. The idle folk in this western world – and there are still a few – are proof of this. They are sad buffoons, perhaps, like the one created by Synge, dependents in spite of themselves of the crushing weight of history. But they are also, necessarily, men of moderation because they are imprisoned in their solitude. Here they sit, these vanquished by Irish fate, in the pubs they love, the unfortunate sons of a noble race. They go in for a pint and then follow it with another, and so they pass the whole day there. They are singular creatures who can be described in several ways – quenched, apathetic, resigned, permanently lost in vague yearnings, suddenly blustering, sprightly and of incomparable verbosity. They stay there for hours, end-lessly discussing in order to drown their boredom; they stay there for hours, pondering in silence over unrealised dreams. They merely wait – for time to pass, for life to pass, for a miracle to happen (no one knows what) to bring the country out of its torpid lethargy. It is a wait without end. A fiddler may arrive, or an accordion-player: then off they go again, warmed on the wings of song, still chasing their dreams. It is customary to point out that over.there on the summit of Croagh Patrick – Ireland's Mount Sinai – one can discern the streets of New York! The songs flow on unchecked, lacerating songs always on the same themes of freedom lost and freedom regained, Ireland and its hurts, Ireland and its heroes, those who have left and those who remain, and the fading dream. As though these orgies of tears could wipe out the infinite pain of this moonstruck land! Faces are unchanging, topped with the same flamboyant hair. And speech is often in the old Gaelic that somehow never quite died out and which, since 1925, the government has been actively trying to revive. Nearly 800,000 Irish are officially registered as Gaelic-speaking – all in the *Gaeltachts* of the western counties where it has remained a living language. But 'progress' comes from the Anglo-Saxon world, painful as this may be for the native tongue.

And so is it still possible to escape the classic dilemma – tradition or survival? Everyday there are people fighting to save the west from the jaws of death, refusing to see it disappear entirely. And, more often than not, they fight without money or means, armed solely with good intentions. Such a man is Father MacDyer who is talked of all over Ireland and who is famous for having tried to revive his parish of Glencolumbkille, at the very bottom of Donegal, in the 1960s. He had two obsessions – to reduce the level of emigration by creating jobs; and to improve the conditions of life by developing local resources. But what a terrible battle he had on his hands! His worst enemies, in his own

Croagh Patrick (County Mayo): the holy mountain and the July pilgrims, barefoot from preference.

The fort of Grianán of
Aileach (County
Donegal). The
omitable spirit of the
ancient Celts.

The enormous beaches of Portnoo in Donegal. They are very highly thought of in this century and are the assets of tomorrow.

words, were 'indifference, emigration, cynicism, greed and individualism'. He took up the challenge with a faith that moved mountains. But how many others are ready and willing to do the same today, before it is too late? A very few, and they only sporadically: and that is the tragedy of these backward rural regions so steeped in conservatism.

They still manage to exist in Donegal, in good and bad years, thanks to a meagre agriculture and to fishing that has been widely developed around Killybegs. Thanks, too, to the home-crafted products of tweed, knitwear and embroidery produced by a thriving cottage industry carried on in the cottages battered by constant storms. The Irish themselves – from Dublin – are beginning to invest around

here and to urbanise this, the world's most archaic coastline, with its wild and savage splendours.

Bloody Foreland, Horn Head, Malin Head and, finally, right in the north, a glimpse of the Hebrides. The Inishowen peninsula with its impressive and peaceful countryside is sublimely beautiful. The fort of **Grianán of Aileach** still stands guard over the northern frontier, a frozen sentinel of the down-trodden Celts. Its sleeping warriors are, according to the legend, waiting to awake for the final battle – the battle that will liberate the whole of Ireland. A people's despair, going beyond Deirdre of the Sorrows, beyond Kathleen ni Houlihan, has concluded by giving birth to the most irrational and crazy hope. *Erin go bra!* Long live Ireland!

6 Ulster-The Great Outdoors

Crossing the border by car from the Republic, the visitor may be forgiven for thinking he has recaptured motoring's glad confident morning. The roads are broad and smooth, the signposts are all in English, and it will cost him less to fill up his tank. But he will also find continuities with the country he has just left.

The highways are remarkably free of traffic, compared with continental Europe or mainland UK, the great skies still move above the fields, the countryside is still green and beautiful, and the same open-handed hospitality for which the whole island is justly famous will greet him in every town and village. As he moves north, he may leave behind a little of the fey charm of the land of leprechauns. He will exchange it for the more robust and sober charm of a region which is rich in scenic, cultural and human interest.

'The north is different.' Who hasn't heard that a hundred times! The *cliché* contains a truth that will resonate at every level among people who understand, think about, or visit Ireland. It expresses a fact about the history of the island, and also reflects the attitudes of many of its inhabitants. An understanding of this difference, alas, is not to be got from contemporary books or from newspapers. Current events in Northern Ireland, and certainly the way in which they have often been manipulated in presentation, have threatened to obscure from view the essential character of this land of lakes and windswept moors, trout streams and well trimmed hedgerows, blue mountains and strangely tinted cliffs. The traveller will be rewarded as he discovers this for himself.

Because Northern Ireland – Ulster as it is often called – has an excellent road system and is only 5000 square miles in area, it is quite realistic for the motorist to visit most of the major attractions within the space of a week, and without clocking up more than 500 miles. A bald list would comprise the following: the historic cities of Belfast, Londonderry and Armagh, each distinctive in character; the coast and glens of Antrim; the Mourne Mountains and the sea lough of Strangford; the inland lakes of Fermanagh; the Sperrin Mountains and the empty moors of western Ulster.

We must start with Belfast, the youngest of the three cities, since this northern metropolis of nearly 400,000 people is still the heart of the Province and was the engine-room that drove the whirring wheels of the industrial revolution which brought such prosperity to Ulster throughout the nineteenth century and far into the twentieth.

The heritage of Northern Ireland, however, is largely a rural one and it is even

Orangemen in their Sunday-go-to-meeting suits: highlight of the 12th July celebrations in Belfast is a huge parade of men on foot. The bands and banners take three hours to pass by.

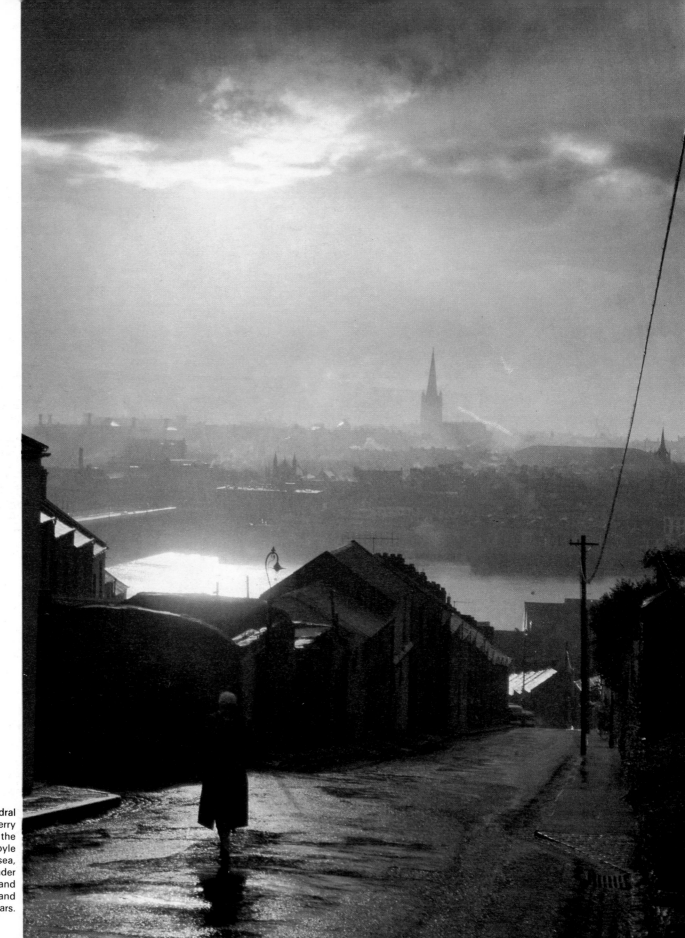

St Columba's Cathedral
dominates the Derry
skyline: rising from the
banks of the river Foyle
and close to the open sea,
the city came under
intermittent siege and
attack for a thousand
years.

now a land of the great outdoors. Ulster people are outdoor people and spend much time on and around the loughs and coastline, fishing or cruising in boats, or simply walking in the mountains and forest parks. All the greater, then, is the visitor's astonishment when, lulled by the sights and small sounds of the countryside, he comes suddenly upon the city.

Unless you approach Belfast from the sea – and it is very much a seaport – you cannot help but come upon the city abruptly because of its spectacular setting. A great grey lozenge, its steel and concrete foundations standing on deep beds of blue mud, and ringed by high hills, sea lough and river valley, this vigorous and very individual city exudes a kind of robust confidence. It has a long tradition of engineering, and the port of Belfast at the head of a deep sea lough has the biggest **ship-building berth** in the world. The giant gantries of the shipyard tower over the south bank of the river Lagan where it meanders to the sea. The core of Northern Ireland's industry is engineering, spreading outwards from Belfast's shipbuilding and aircraft industries but including a great number of small engineering shops.

Hemmed in by the countryside, the city itself is extremely compact and, despite the ravages of the Second World War, the planners and the terrorists, is still full of self-assertive, exuberant Victorian and Edwardian architecture with elaborate sculptures over doors and windows. The fine city hall, built at the turn of the century, has been much mocked, not least by the citizens of Belfast. It sits four-square like a great white wedding cake, dominating the city centre, an impressive building full of civic pride. Half a century and half a mile separates it from Queen's University which, with its mellow brickwork, Tudor cloister and mullioned windows, has quite another style. The main college building was modelled on Magdalen

Hidden high in the Mountains of Mourne: deep blue little Lough Shannagh.

College, Oxford, and indeed, with its proud academic tradition, the university has remained a centre of excellence and sanity, regarded with affection by all the citizens of Belfast throughout 'the Troubles'.

Northern Ireland's second city, Londonderry, has a long and tumultuous history. Set on a hill on the banks of the Foyle estuary and placed strategically close to the open sea, the city came under intermittent siege and attack for a thousand years. The name Derry comes from the Irish *Doire* – 'a place of oaks' – and named after the tree-crowned hill on which St Columba founded his first abbey in 546.

The best way to see Londonderry is to walk right round the unbroken seventeenth century walls which withstood three sieges, the final one lasting

105 days when the forces of James II failed to take the 'Maiden City'. Six metres thick, the walls are said to be the last city walls to be built in Europe. Unfortunately, the full circuit cannot be made at present since some sections are controlled by the security forces. Within the walls are a number of fine churches, perhaps the most notable being **St Columba's Cathedral** in 'Planters' Gothic' style. Inside, the cathedral walls are hung with plaques that commemorate Derry's London connections, and in the porch is a stone inscription:

'If stones could speake then London's prayse should sounde
Who built this church and cittie from the grounde.'

At the time of the Plantation of Ulster, the City of London sent masterbuilders

and money to rebuild the ruined mediaeval town – hence the name Londonderry. The chapterhouse is full of memories of the city's tumultuous history, including the keys of the gates which were shut against the army of James II by the Apprentice Boys.

The main thoroughfare of the city, Shipquay Street, is exceptionally steep, with many narrow little streets running off it; and from the quay behind the Guildhall, hundreds of thousands of Irish emigrants sailed to the New World, including the Scotch-Irish ancestors of future American presidents.

The last and oldest of the three cities, Armagh, has a more tranquil past. Dominated by two cathedrals that stand on adjoining hills, it has been the ecclesiastical capital of Ireland for 1500 years. The Anglican cathedral occupies the site where St Patrick is thought to have built his church, and the **Catholic cathedral** has an impressive west front with tall twin spires. With its marble pavements and fine town houses, the city has an air of quiet dignity. It rises south-west of rich fruit-growing country which has earned for Armagh the name of the 'garden of Ulster'. The area is at its most beautiful in May when the apple blossom is heavy on the trees. Enough of urban things! If the city is the most lasting and the most inspiring expression of men's social genius, surely the country is its cradle. Ways of escape out to the fresh air of the countryside are quick and numerous. To reach the Antrim Coast from Belfast, it is simple to go by the shore road to Larne by way of Carrickfergus Castle; built on a rocky spur of hard volcanic rock, this well preserved Norman castle has a commanding site guarding Belfast Lough. Now a regimental museum, it was in military occupation for more than seven centuries.

The stretch of coastline totalling about 60 miles between Larne and

could imagine. In many ways it is reminiscent of the spectacular Californian Highway One that runs from Santa Barbara to San Francisco. The visitor is advised to begin from the Larne end, rather than from Portrush since some of the best features remain hidden from view if approached from the west. All along the eastern part, as far as Ballycastle, there is always the

... to colonists who would change the course of history. The ruins of Dunluce Castle (County Antrim), a Scottish fief dating from the Elizabethan era.

Portrush is the most beautiful that one could imagine. In many ways it is temptation to turn inland to explore the Glens of Antrim, a series of nine valleys formed some 20,000 years ago by retreating glaciers. The best known is the green valley of Glenariff with its waterfalls and broad-leaved woodland by the river. Of exceptional interest to geologists, the coastline is a veritable textbook illustrating the geological story of the earth. Flows of molten lava buried a whole series of older rocks and protected them from atmospheric destruction. These old rocks now jut out as cliffs along the edge of the plateau in all their brilliant colours. There are

One of the mysterious Janus idols in Caldragh cemetery on Boa Island in Lower Lough Erne (County Fermanagh). From pagan gods ...

bright red sandstones, white chalk, black basalt and blue clays.

Fair Head, the north-eastern extremity of the coast, has 16 different strata in its 200 metres of scarped headland, including basalt, sandstone, coal and iron ore. From the summit there is a wonderful view of the whole of Rathlin Island, six miles out, and of the hills and islands of Scotland 13 miles away across the narrow North Channel; Kintyre, Aran, Jura, Ailsa Craig and Galloway can all be seen. Beneath the headland on the east side lie the silky sands and wooded slopes of Murlough Bay.

Between Fair Head and Magilligan Point, some 45 miles away where a beach seven miles long curves round

at the entrance to Lough Foyle, lie a myriad hidden coves and little bays, deep caves and romantic ruins.

Rathlin Island, six miles in extent, is shaped like a sock, with the toe pointing back towards the mainland. Its white cliffs are the haunt of sea birds and host to wild flowers. In about 1800, the island had a human population of more than a thousand. Now there are only 30 families who mostly raise cattle and sell fish. Herring, mackerel, pollack, plaice, flounder and other flatfish are plentiful round the coast. Deep-sea anglers take cod, haddock, skate and other big fish – and sharks have been seen off the north coast. Although the island is almost completely treeless, there is a wealth of

wild flowers, seapinks, milkweed, tree-mallows, small orchids and primroses. Robert the Bruce hid in a cave on Rathlin in 1306 after his defeat by the English at Perth, and it was a Rathlin spider whose arachnoid energies gave the despondent warrior new heart and sent him back to Scotland to win the Battle of Bannockburn.

West along Fair Head past Bally-

Carrick-a-Rede (County Antrim). In the hollow of the cliffs, an islet rich in salmon, linked to the mainland by a rope bridge.

The Giant's Causeway and its astonishing complex of 37,000 basalt columns. A natural feature whose beauty has sprung from the mind of men.

castle, one of the most attractive seaside places on the Antrim coast, the Carrick-a-Rede Rope Bridge links the land to a small rocky island over a 26 metres chasm. Made of planks strung between wires, the bridge is used by salmon fishermen to reach their fishery house.

White Park Bay, protected by the National Trust, is a crescent of white beach in a grassy bowl of dunes and cliffs, with the tiny hamlet of Portbraddan tucked into a cleft in the cliffs. The hamlet has an even tinier church with a thatched roof. It was built by a local resident who dedicated it to St Gobhan, patron saint of builders.

Further west, past the ruins of Dunseverick Castle on the cliff edge, the strange and wonderful rock formation of the **Giant's Causeway** begins, or rather ends, since its most spectacular manifestation is at the other end of a coastal path provided by the National Trust from the entrance to the Causeway to beyond Dunseverick. The Causeway proper is an astonishing complex of basalt columns packed tightly together; the

Ireland's best preserved round tower stands sentinel on Devenish Island in Lower Lough Erne. From its high windows, the island monks espied approaching strangers. In its cool cavities, they rang their bells and hid their sacred relicts.

tops of the columns form stepping stones leading from the cliff foot and disappearing under the sea. There are similar columns on the island of Staffa in the Hebrides and hence the legend that this was a highway built by a giant from Ireland to Scotland. So close an affinity is there – both historical and spiritual – between this coastline and the beckoning hills of Scotland, that the visitor contemplating this wide, commodious, truncated highway may feel somewhat regretful that such a picturesque route to Scotland is not available to him today. Over the Causeway as a whole, there are about 37,000 of these stone columns, mostly hexagonal but some with four, five, seven and eight sides. The tallest are about 13 metres high, and the solidified lava in the cliffs is in places 26 metres thick.

Midway between the Causeway and Portrush is the romantic silhouette of ruined **Dunluce Castle.** Poised above the sea on an isolated crag, the castle is reached by a wooden bridge that replaces the former drawbridge. A large cave leads right through the rock under the castle out to the sea and served as a secret entry and exit. The first stone castle was built by the Norman Richard de Burgh in about 1300, although there was certainly an ancient Irish fort on the site before then. The castle often came under siege and in 1584 the Irish recaptured it from the English when one of their number, employed in the castle, hauled men up the cliff in a basket by night. A strong gatehouse and two round flanking towers are all that remain, teetering on the edge of the cliff.

Three miles south of the Causeway is the small town of Bushmills, noted for its ancient whiskey distillery, and also for salmon and trout fishing on the river Bush. The first licence to distil whiskey here was granted in 1609 though it is good to know that *usquebaugh*, the 'water of life', had sustained the locals for a fair number of

centuries before then.

At Portrush, with its two long beaches and two 18-hole golf courses, the Antrim Coast, strictly speaking, comes to an end; but just next door is the magnificent two miles long sandy beach of Portstewart, County Londonderry's main seaside resort, where motorists can (and some, apparently, prefer this to walking) drive along the firm sand towards the mouth of the river Bann.

Across the Bann is Downhill Castle, the palatial cliff-top demesne of Frederick Hervey, fourth Earl of Bristol and Bishop of Derry, a flamboyant eighteenth century nobleman who

built three great houses of varying degrees of extravagance, and travelled Europe collecting works of art to fill them. He planted thousands of trees and made a walled garden on the bleak headland, with fishponds and a dovecote. Inviting a friend to visit Downhill, the Bishop wrote, 'Come and enjoy . . . the success with which I have converted 60 acres of moor, by the medium of two hundred spades, into a green carpet sprinkled with white clover!' Today the castle is open to the winds but, a short walk from the ruins, on the edge of the cliff is perched a small and exquisite circular temple, the Mussenden Temple which by some

Trout fishing on the tranquil river Main near Cullybackey (County Antrim).

miracle and now with a little help from the National Trust, stands intact. The Bishop, a man of great generosity and some piety, made strenuous efforts to heal the political and religious dissensions in Ireland. Medical science, at that time, was not sufficiently advanced to establish whether it was these efforts that made him go mad, or whether his mental instability later in life had some other cause.

County Down, which bounds Belfast on the south, as does County Antrim to the north, has a strikingly different landscape, or rather series of landscapes. The northern part is the country of drumlins – hillocks of glacial clay that look like an upturned egg carton – which have also produced many of the islands in the great sea lough of Strangford. To the east are the fishing villages and smooth beaches of the Ards Peninsula, and beyond and above the south are the compact blue cones of the much celebrated **Mourne Mountains.**

The curiously regular shape of the tightly packed, steep-sided little hills called drumlins gives north Down a distinctly odd appearance. Driving along the road between Saintfield and Killinchy, for instance, is rather like travelling along a switchback; the car is propelled through a series of dips and rises in such rapid succession that one hardly needs to brake or accelerate. This is rich agricultural land, and the whole district is highly cultivated;

Strangford Lough: summer breeding grounds for sea birds, the vast sea lough gives winter sanctuary to Greenland's geese.

many of the drumlins have neat hedges and fences running up their steep sides; some are bright green, others are brown, and some are coloured by the particular crop being grown. This strange bumpy patchwork is a unique characteristic of Down.

Strangford Lough is also part of drumlin country, except that the land, being lower, has been invaded by the sea to make an archipelago. Scores of drowned drumlins pop up here and there, mostly near the shore, and many of the flatter islands were drumlins until they were eroded by the sea. These islands give the lough the appearance of a freshwater lough, at least from the sheltered northern end, some 18 miles from the narrow entrance, less than half a mile wide, that connects it to the Irish Sea at the south end. Four hundred million tons of water rush through the gap twice a day, and the Vikings named it 'violent fjord' (Strangford) after the fierce currents in these tidal narrows. The lough is a great bird sanctuary and the whole of the inner foreshore has been designated a wildlife and ornithological reserve. A large flock of brent geese – the pale-breasted variety that breed in north-east Greenland – winters here, and greylag and white-fronted geese often visit from the Downpatrick marshes. Whooper swans gather in the north-east corner in the winter and the mudflats attract a wide variety of waders, including redshank, oyster-catchers and curlews. Summer residents include many kinds of tern and gulls who breed on islands on the western side. Herons and hooded crows breed on some of the bigger islands, along with finches and robins. The lough also has a rich marine life, including a hundred different species of fish. Seals are often seen basking on the lower islands, and sea hares, sun stars and curled octopus sometimes appear on the shore. With such a wealth of readily available food, it is not surprising that the lough

The Catholic Cathedral of St Patrick in Armagh, the holy city of Ireland since its conversion and the spiritual capital of both communities.

Spotless inside and often rainbow-painted outside, Ulster's 'Coronation Streets' are earmarked for redevelopment.

is occasionally visited by predators like the rare buzzard, sparrowhawks and short-eared owls. There are also good pickings for foxes who lurk along the tide-lines at night in search of roosting wildfowl, and otters and stoats come visiting, with the same sinister intent, in hard winters.

All round the 20 miles long lough are interesting and historic places. For example, Mount Stewart House on the eastern shore, the birthplace of Castlereagh, Foreign Secretary of

England during the Napoleonic wars, has a large garden that was redesigned and replaced by the Marchioness of Londonderry earlier this century. She designed an elaborate topiary garden for her children and filled it with fantastic statues of dodos and dinosaurs for their amusement. Further down the lough at Grey Abbey are the well preserved ruins of a twelfth century Cistercian abbey with a profusion of trees and rare flowers in the grounds.

The two roads that run the length of the Ards Peninsula on its opposite shores could not be more different. And yet it is a matter of a few minutes to cross, at Grey Abbey, from one of these worlds to the other, from the sheltered, almost land-locked, lough where wildfowl nest, to burst upon the rollers of the open sea. The road runs south past the harbours and through the white-washed fishing villages, past Portavogie harbour where seals bob against the prawn boats as the catch is landed, to Portaferry village at Strangford's tidal narrows.

The long waterfront at Portaferry is a delightful combination of terraced cottages, Georgian and early Victorian town houses, and a harmonious terrace of new cottages that shows modern domestic architecture at its best. The ferryboat to Strangford village leaves from the slipway opposite Queen's University Marine Biology Station, and to cross the swift narrows at Portaferry is to get yet one more perspective on the wooded and winding lough shores.

The melody and the words – 'Where the Mountains of Mourne sweep down to the sea' – of the popular song have ensured that these are the best known mountains in Ireland although they are not the highest. Tucked away in the south-east extremity of Ulster, with their high domes and smooth profiles, they are distinctive and self-contained in an area of about 15 miles by eight miles. In the eastern half of the range there are 12 rounded summits rising above 650 metres. No road reaches the wilderness at the centre and so they have a special magnetism for the walker, but the good roads round their circumference mean that the motorist can enjoy constantly changing panoramas of peaks, and he can drive up to the Silent Valley, though he must make arrangements in advance with the appropriate authority. The mountains are bounded on the east and south by the sea and the north-eastern part is sharply defined. To the west they taper off

Belfast: the shipyards and the port. Ships as far as the eye can see. A far-flung industrial complex.

Go West, young man! John Dunlap, printer of the American Declaration of Independence, learned his trade on Gray's printing press at Strabane (County Tyrone).

into Brontë country round Banbridge and Newry. The simplest way to conceive the high Mournes is in the shape of an M, the right-hand prong being the wide Annalong river valley and the left prong the Silent Valley. Along the top of the M runs the Brandy Pad, the old smugglers' track, bisected by the dramatic Hare's Gap. The two big artificial lakes in the Silent Valley are the water reservoirs for Belfast and several other towns, supplying over six million litres

The cottier's house: buildings from Ulster's rural past have been reconstructed at the Folk Museum, Cultra (County Down).

of water a day. The catchment area is encircled by a massive dry stone wall, two metres high, which ascends and descends the high peaks surrounding the inner Mournes.

The highest peak, barren Slieve Donard, which rises steeply to 930 metres within two miles of Dundrum Bay, can easily be climbed in an afternoon from Bloody Bridge near Newcastle. Extravagant claims about what can be seen from the tops of mountains are all too common and there is nothing more annoying for the normally unathletic seeker-after-truth than struggling to a mountain top and not seeing the things that one is said to be able to see on a clear day. However, an ever-improving view of the Isle of Man, clearly visible out to sea, accompanies the toiler on the way up Slieve Donard's steep sides, and the view from the top is superb. You can see all of County Down and the whole length of Strangford Lough with Scrabo Tower at its head. To the north are the Belfast hills, with the pale line of Lough Neagh to the north-west. It is said that on a lucky day you can also see the Scottish coast, Snowdon in Wales, the Cumbrian hills of England and the mountains of Donegal.

The coast from Newcastle to the hamlet of Greencastle at the mouth of Carlingford Lough was famous for smuggling in the eighteenth century and still has many coastguard lookout points. Wines and spirits, tobacco, tea, silk and soap were brought across from the Isle of Man in small boats and taken along the Brandy Pad through the mountains to Hilltown in the western foothills of the Mournes. Newcastle itself, once the coastguards' headquarters, is now the biggest seaside resort in the east Down. There is yachting and pleasure fishing from the old harbour, with golf on the fine courses of the Royal County Down Gold Club and still unspoiled sand dunes. The huge Norman keep at Greencastle was built by the Anglo-Normans in the thirteenth century – at about the same time as Carlingford Castle across the lough – to guard this major sea access to Ulster. In the Middle Ages, Greencastle was the biggest settlement of the little Kingdom of Mourne, the thin strip of coastal land that runs south from Newcastle to Carlingford Lough, isolated from the rest of Ulster by the Mournes, and still something of a law unto itself.

The watery, forested county of Fermanagh lies in the limestone basin of the River Erne which meanders from end to end of the county, in no hurry to reach the sea. It is difficult to be precise about the number of lakes in Fermanagh but there are 154 islands on the biggest lake, Lough Erne, which is over 50 miles long. The lake has a small constriction in the middle where the county town of Enniskillen stands. A paradise for birds and wild flowers, it is also a magnet for anglers, especially for coarse fishing but also for brown trout and salmon, and more recently, for cruising. Good hotels, tackle shops and hire boats provide what visitors expect – particularly German visitors: so many Germans are now coming here that some of the locals are making strenuous efforts to learn German. The lakeside is high and rocky in many places and, apart from the islands, there are dozens of coves and inlets to explore. The lough is ideal cruising water and, in fact, it is better to explore Fermanagh by boat than by car, though there are excellent roads, with lakeside picnic sites, and good views too. Lower Lough Erne, running for 26 miles almost to the Atlantic, is six miles wide in places and very unlike labyrinthine Upper Lough Erne. When the winds blow, navigation can become something of a challenge, with waves of open-sea dimensions. Shallow Upper Lough Erne, flowing south-east of the town for about 12 miles, narrows to under a quarter of a mile here and there; it so proliferates with islands that the navigator needs a chart to find his way.

With such a site, you would expect Enniskillen to be an historic town of great antiquity and it is. Its origins go back to pre-history when this short nexus must have been the main high-

The 'crystallised history' for which Ulster is famous: primitive politico-religious paintings on gable ends, like this long-vanished one of George VI, are fast disappearing beneath the developers' bulldozers.

Mourne country: the central wilderness is accessible only on foot or on horseback.

way between the lands to the north and the lands to the south. It has had its share too of more recent history. It was the scene of a legion of battles and, before the Ulster Plantation in the seventeenth century, was the chief place of the Maguires, chieftains of Fermanagh. Their castle still stands. In later centuries, the town's fame derived mainly from the valiant deeds of the Royal Inniskilling Fusiliers and the Inniskilling Dragoons who fought at Waterloo. Relics of the Enniskillen regiments can be seen in the museum in Maguire's Castle.

On a hill on the western fringes of the town is Portora Royal School established by James I in 1608. Oscar Wilde went to school at Portora and so did Samuel Beckett. In the school gardens are the ruins of Portora Castle which was blown up by experimenting school-boys in 1859.

On Devenish Island, a couple of miles from Enniskillen on the lower lake, a twelfth century **round tower** – the best preserved, most complete, in Ireland – stands sentinel, and there are some extensive remains of early to mediaeval

Christian settlements. Islands were favourite monastery sites because of their seclusion and comparative safety, especially from marauding Vikings. The foundation of a monastery on Devenish is attributed to St Molaise in the sixth century, and the book shrine of Molaise, which is one of the masterpieces of Irish Christian art and may have been made on Devenish, is now in the National Museum, Dublin. The Augustinian Abbey of St Mary, on the higher part of the island, has beautifully carved doorways on the tower and sacristy. In the cemetery on Boa Island, another fascinating and historic island on the lower lough, there are two ancient stone looking-both-ways Janus idols. Believed to date from the first century, they probably survived the long years because Boa remained a druid's sanctuary after Ireland became Christian. White Island and Inishmacsaint also have their *numen*, as befits sacred islands, the first having a collection of inscrutable Christian statues of distinctly pagan mien; and the second, a cross over four metres high with flared arms, and a herd of goats running wild.

Mary McDonnell's pub, Ballycastle: the whiskey comes from Bushmills, the world's oldest distillery, west along the Antrim coast.

Below the lake, passing the little village of Belleek, where the pottery produces lustrous porcelain *objets*, the Erne river at last plunges into a gorge to meet the Atlantic.

Both of Northern Ireland's motorways strike out west from Belfast, skirting Lough Neagh, 'that noble sheet of water', to the north and the south. By taking either route, the surfeited traveller in search of solitude can reach the empty spaces of central Ulster. By way of Lisburn and Dungannon, the M1 will take him to the empty moorlands of south Tyrone. To the north, the wide M2 heads towards the Sperin Mountains. Threaded by streams and small roads, this range of gentle contours is bounded by the towns of Magherafelt, Cookstown, Dungannon, Omagh and Strabane. Within this charmed circle few people live today, though this has not always been so. The thousand standing stones across the range are the extant testimony of the Stone Age people who inhabited these empty places.

Neither the scars of political dissatisfaction nor the years of sectarian violence will diminish the newcomer's surprised delight at being in the presence of an elemental beauty and an infinite variety of waters, skies and landscapes when he first travels to the Province of Northern Ireland.

Seamus Heaney, the Ulster poet, in good voice at the Queen's University Festival, Belfast.

The Peace People: the phenomenal rallies of the mid-seventies have melted away but the work goes quietly on.

Malin Head

Horn Head

Giants Causeway

Bloody Foreland

▲ Errigal 750 m

Londonderry

● Coleraine

ANTRIM

LONDONDERRY

Bann

● Larne

DONEGAL

TYRONE

● Omagh

U L S T E R

Lough Neagh

● **BELFAST**

● Donegal

DONEGAL BAY

Lower
Lough Erne

● Dungannon

DOWN

● Enniskillen

● Armagh

● Downpatrick

LEITRIM

FERMANAGH

ARMAGH

● Sligo

Upper Lough Erne

● Newry

The Mullet

SLIGO

Lough Allen

MONAGHAN

● Ballina

CAVAN

LOUTH

● Dundalk

MAYO

Carrick-on-Shannon

Achill Island

ROSCOMMON

● Kells

MEATH

● Drogheda

CLEW BAY

● Westport

C O N N A C H T

LONGFORD

● Tara

Croagh Patrick 750 m ▲

● Trim

Killary Harbour

● Lough Mask

Boyne

● Clifden

Lough Ree

● Mullingar

Connemara

Lough Corrib

● Athlone

WEST MEATH

DUBLIN

GALWAY

● **DUBLIN**

Galway ●

Liffey

GALWAY BAY

Shannon

OFFALY

KILDARE

L E I N S T E R

Aran Islands

LEIX

WICKLOW

Cliffs of Moher

Burren

Lough Derg

Barrow

● Ennis

Slaney

CLARE

TIPPERARY

CARLOW

● Kilkenny

Loop Head

Limerick

● Enniscorthy

MOUTH OF THE SHANNON

Sur

KILKENNY

WEXFORD

Kerry Head

● Tipperary

● Cashel

● Wexford

LIMERICK

● Clonmel

● Tralee

M U N S T E R

Waterford

Carnsore Point

Blasket Islands

● Mallow

WATERFORD

Blackwater

Saltee Islands

DINGLE BAY

● Killarney

Lee

● Youghal

Skellig Rocks

▲ Carrantuohill 1040 m

CORK

KERRY

Cork ●

● Glengarriff

● Kinsale

KENMARE RIVER

BANTRY BAY

● Skibbereen

Mizen Head

Cape Clear

0   40   80

Km

APPENDICES

by Françoise Bonnefoy,
Brigitte Logeart
and Annie Perrier-Robert

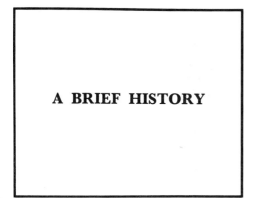

A BRIEF HISTORY

How is it possible to relate the history of this land of poetry, folly and death in only a few lines? Green Erin, the Emerald Isle, with its contrasting country-sides, the land of legends, of lovers asleep on the dolmens, the country of steppes and wild ponies, of blue hills and dry-stone walls, of moving skies, mountain streams and lakes, of dazzling white walls crowned with thatch, of carefree donkeys and opulent cows, of pink rhododendrons beside tumuli . . . surrounded by the whimsical ocean and the calm sea . . . strife-torn Ireland whose fate began its uneven course several centuries ago when the Anglo-Normans wished to conquer it. . . .

There is very little known precisely about when man first appeared in Ireland, only that it happened relatively late, perhaps some time around 9000 B.C. During the Mesolithic Age (about 6800 B.C.) men originating in the south-west of Scotland settled in the north-east of Ireland, in present-day Ulster, (in Antrim and Down). They slowly made their way through the forest towards the south by way of the east coast. About 3500 B.C. settlers – who were purely hunters – were there in no great number. Then new waves of them arrived – this time they were farmers. In the Neolithic Age (around 2500 B.C.) civilisation began to develop. Agriculture became more widespread with the cultivation of barley and corn; the farmers began to rear animals and the pig, cow and sheep joined the already domesticated dog. Weaving and pottery-making developed. In the clearings the 'peasants' began to group together in villages. This was also the apogee of the great megalithic fever and menhirs, dolmens and cromlechs were erected nearly everywhere. In the Boyne valley there is a veritable 'complex' of princely tombs, the most impressive being Newgrange, Dowth and Knowth.

Ireland prospered in the Bronze Age because it possessed copper and gold mines. The inhabitants resembled Mediterranean-dwellers, being brown and small in stature. In the sixth century B.C. the Celts, greedy for wealth, invaded the country and imposed their La Tène civilisation upon it. Ireland was fragmented into small realms (*túatha*) ruled by an elected king, a patriarch, warchief and judge. Society was strongly hierarchical with slaves, bonds-men and freemen, but national unity was safe-guarded by the druids who spread a common language and literary, historical and judicial traditions. It proved difficult to elect a 'High King' (*Árd Rígh*) who had authority over the whole of Ireland. The claims put forward by the king of Tara (the capital of Leinster) for possession of this title only appeared at a relatively late stage. Wars, combats and raids on cattle increased from *túath* to *túath*, from clan to clan, and formed the crucible for the epic cycles: one of the most ancient being the *Táin Bó Cúaulnge*, telling of the prowess of Cuchu-lain, the hero of Ulster and the Irish Achilles.

When Christianity reached Ireland it was already split into five rival kingdoms, having been outside the bounds of the Roman Empire. This fragmenta-tion and internal strife was to remain a charac-teristic of the country throughout its subsequent history. But Ireland's conversion by St Patrick nevertheless transformed it completely and forever. Patrick was born around A.D. 385 in the north of Roman Britain. He was captured by Gaelic pirates and became the slave of a druid from whom he managed to escape. When he discovered the Christian God he took a vow that he would convert Ireland and he went back in 432, having been sent there by Pope Celestine. He was scarcely 30 years old when he won the country for Christ. The Picts (the most ancient dwellers in Ireland) and the Celts had now united and there were no longer any but the Goidels (Gaels), the men of Ireland. The slave class disappeared. When St Patrick died in 461 the country was covered in churches. Half a century later the Church had become Celtic and monastic, although it started life as episcopal and Roman. The monastery corresponded to the rural and tribal framework of Irish society. Its organisation was closely copied from the family structure and its lifestyle was allied to that of the tribe. In the Mero-vingian and Carolingian era Ireland became the refuge for learned men passionately in search of knowledge. Rediscovered manuscripts adorned with abstract patterns of inspired curves and spirals bear witness to the survival of Celtic art. From the sixth century onwards the latinate and Celtic cul-tures enhanced each other by intertwining and the saints were attributed the qualities of legendary heroes. . . . Sheltered from the barbarian invasions rampaging on the continent during the seventh and eighth centuries, Ireland experienced a golden age. The country was to play an initiatory role in the intellectual 'renaissance' of the high Middle Ages. The monastic 'cities' – Clonard, Clonmacnoise, Armagh, Glendalough – overflowed with Breton noblemen and Merovingian princes. The monks themselves spread virtually everywhere, evangelis-ing Germania, founding monasteries in Scotland, France and Italy. Tutors and teachers of current thought in barbaric Europe, they reached the Faroes, Iceland and even America. . . .

But, like all blessed ages, the golden age could not last. The Norwegians and Danes undertook to break it during the ninth and tenth centuries. In the course of manifold raids the country was ravaged and the abbeys devastated. Then the Vikings settled on various parts of the coast establishing bases from which the first Irish towns grew up. Dublin, Wicklow, Wexford, Waterford, Cork and Limerick originated in this way. The 'barbarian' occupation was made simpler by the internal struggles in Ire-land. Some of the kings allied themselves with the invaders against their rivals. It was a troubled period from which Ireland, nevertheless, drew a certain amount of good; the country had been exclusively rural and pastoral until that time and now it learnt about commerce and the use of silver as currency. And it was in the very first years of the eleventh century that Ireland even experienced the first inklings of national 'unity', under the leader-ship of Brian Boru, who succeeded in defeating the Vikings at the battle of Clontarf in 1014, though he was himself killed.

Should one hold the subsequent rivalry between the High Kings of Ireland, Dermot MacMurrough and Rory O'Connor, responsible for the English occupation of the country? Or was it because of a papal bull issued by Hadrian IV giving Ireland to Henry Plantagenet, King of England, Duke of Aquitaine and Normandy? In 1169 the armoured Normans, led by Richard Clare, Earl of Pembroke (and known as Strongbow) landed near Wexford and marched on Dublin. Henry II himself landed at Waterford and received the island's submission at Cashel. This conquest did not become completely effective until the sixteenth century.

Three-quarters of the country was in the hands of the conquerors from the middle of the thirteenth century. Fortified castles were built and wealthy towns grew up around them. Trade with the conti-nent developed. The Irish were not wiped out, merely reduced to the state of 'villeins'. In the face of such changes the Celts roused themselves and likewise began to build impressive stone castles; they joined forces and rebelled. The territory under total Anglo-Norman domination – the Pale – was reduced to a narrow coastal strip from Dublin to Dundalk. On the other hand, some Norman barons got on extremely well with the 'red-headed' girls. But the kings of England were worried by this newly developing baronial power and the gradual 'Celticisation' of the old English colonists whose interests became less and less those of England: they spoke Gaelic, used the old Brehon law, dressed like the Irish and became 'more Irish than the Irish themselves'. The Kilkenny Statutes were passed in 1366 to combat this undesirable tendency.

The power of the monarch was restored in England in the fifteenth century and soon deter-mined that country's attitude towards an oligarchic, 'anarchic' Ireland that threatened the status of royalty. It was necessary to 'pacify' it. Henry VII despatched his 'special envoy', Poynings, to do the job. Was this a fraud or a skilful trick? This the Drogheda parliament was to show in 1494 with its well-known laws that stayed in force until the end of the eighteenth century: the Irish parliament could not meet again without the consent of the English king; its legislation was subject to that of London.

But was there a spark, a delicate shadow of the beginning of entente between Ireland and the formidable Henry VIII? In 1541 the first Dublin parliament proclaimed Henry VIII King of Ire-land. But, like the majority of love-matches, it did not last. Ireland would not accept the Reformation that this monarch tried to impose and the country rose against him. Repression came swiftly and with cruel savagery. A colonising policy – or rather a policy of 'plantation' – was applied. Under the Catholic Queen Mary Tudor two counties were assigned to Protestant English colonists. The end of the sixteenth century, the age of Elizabeth I was fearful. Rebellions led by the Earls Desmond, O'Neill and O'Donnell, who held Munster, Ulster and Connacht, were mercilessly put down. The new and affluent colonists despised the old Celtic customs. Ulster became a Presbyterian stronghold of ardent non-Conformists. Celts and Celticised Anglo-Normans pitted themselves against the growing numbers of colonists: the latter felt threatened and, supported by the English parliament, determined to repress the Irish. In the first years of the seventeenth century the 'flight of the earls' after the fall of Kinsale, marked the end of the Irish aristocracy. The 'plantations' flourished and grew more numerous. In 1641 the shock of rebellion in England shook the whole of Ireland. In 1649 and 1650 Cromwell and his Ironsides landed on the 'little island'. Cruelty and terror ensued, the massacres of Drogheda and Wexford ... then Cromwell and his troops returned to England. In spite of everything the war continued, until 1652. Then a 'pacification' Act intervened, the Cromwellian Settlement under which all the indigenous Irish had to leave their possessions in Ulster, Leinster and Munster and exile themselves in 'hell or Connacht'. Officers and soldiers of the crown took possession of the confiscated lands and the dispossessed peasantry became their 'serfs'.

The Restoration of Charles II, then James II, sowed seeds of hope in the hearts of the Irish, but they had little chance of germinating. The Catholic kings of England were controlled by their Protestant subjects and could, therefore, give back only a few lands and assign a few posts in the army and the government. These minor concessions were swept aside when William of Orange, the Protestant son-in-law of James II, came to the throne. William gathered his supporters in Ireland, fought and won the battle of the Boyne in 1690 and James II fled to France. Londonderry and Eniskillin were besieged by Catholics and the resistance of the Protestants in the former (for four months) was memorable.

The town of Limerick held out against the English for a year and finally offered to surrender itself in exchange for toleration for the Catholics to the degree allowed by Charles II. This contract was broken by a London parliament which wanted to prove its authority in Ireland to the Protestant English colonists. The Catholics were expelled from the Dublin parliament, the Irish nobility and bourgeoisie disappeared and more lands were confiscated. All the men were reduced to the state of farmers under the great English landowners. The whole of Irish trade had to be carried on from England; in particular wool had to be exported and it was forbidden to spin it locally. At each bad harvest the poorest classes were attacked by famine and misery. In 1695 the Penal Code took away from the Catholics their last remaining civil and religious rights: they could no longer vote, nor were they allowed to enter the army, the navy or the liberal professions or be called to the bar; they were forbidden the right of instruction and the clergy had to take an oath of loyalty to the Crown. Nevertheless, despite these restricting conditions, the population of Ireland grew from two to four million inhabitants in the course of the eighteenth century.

Eamon De Valera in 1914.

Charles Stewart Parnell.

Secret societies grew up; the White boys, the Oak Boys, hardly worrying the English government. But common interests reunited the Catholics and the Protestants. Gradually a national Irish spirit took shape, nurtured by the Anglican minority who were also oppressed by the British government. And the Dublin parliament, although it was made up solely of Protestants, defended the interests of the 'Irish nation'.

In 1775 the American War of Independence gave Ireland the chance to make itself heard, after the British troops stationed there left the island. In 1778 the Dublin parliament raised a militia of 75,000 men, when French invasion seemed imminent, to resist it. With the backing of this force the 'patriotic party' inspired by the Protestant lawyer, Henry Grattan, obtained freedom of trade. In 1782 the Penal Laws were rescinded in favour of the Gardiner laws. In 1783 the London parliament recognised the autonomy of the Dublin parliament. But religious differences flared up again. The wealthy Catholics were finally given the right to vote and to enter the professions in 1793. A French invasion at Bantry Bay in 1796 was a failure. Wolfe Tone, at the head of the Society of United Irishmen, led uprisings in 1791 and 1798, without success. The reprisals were fearsome.

The Irish rebellion presented a crucial dilemma for England. There was a state of anarchy. What was the best method to adopt in order to cope with the problems of a majority of poor Catholics subjected to several thousand wealthy Protestants – the Ascendancy, who held more than half the land? Only one solution seemed possible – the union of the two nations, that would at least give England direct control over the country. The Act of Union was passed in 1800 following the wishes of Pitt, and against widespread opposition. The Dublin parliament disappeared. Twenty-eight peers, four bishops and a hundred members of Commons were to represent Ireland in Parliament. The Catholic hopes of obtaining emancipation (promised by Pitt) were disappointed when George III refused to permit it and Pitt resigned. A movement claiming these rights was started under the leadership of Daniel O'Connell, a young Catholic lawyer. O'Connell was intelligent and skilful enough to keep the fight on a legal footing, causing a current of sympathy for Ireland to flow in England. In April 1829 he succeeded in his aim and the London government granted to Catholics eligibility and access to all public offices. For ten years, between 1830 and 1840, there were mass demonstrations against the Union, although these were severely punished, and the Catholics gathered under the banner of the Young Ireland Party, whose leaders advocated violence.

The Irish economy could only get worse. Ireland began to feel the competition of America in the corn market. From 1846 to 1849 a terrible famine was caused by the bad harvest resulting from the rain and the blights that attacked the potatoes, the staple diet of the Irish peasantry. Typhus, cholera, dysentery and scurvy attacked the already-weakened and desperate population. The workshops created by the English minister, Robert Peel, to combat unemployment, were swamped then abandoned and the repeal of the Corn Laws came too late for many Irish. Thousands left their native land

The Mussenden Temple, Downhill, County Londonderry: built by the fourth Earl of Bristol and Bishop of Derry, the temple was inspired by the temples of Vesta at Tivoli in Rome.

Hillsborough Fort, County Down: rebuilt as a place of entertainment in the eighteenth century by the powerful Hill family, the old fort dates from 1630.

Intact eighteenth century corn mill at Ballycopeland, Millisle, County Down: before the industrial revolution, ingenious mechanisms of wood and iron used only the wind to grind the people's corn.

The Mellon Homestead, Camphill, County Tyrone: the family emigrated to start a new life in America in 1818. Judge Thomas Mellon of Pittsburgh was born in this humble cottage in 1813.

for the United States and Canada. Others died from poverty and exhaustion. By 1851 the unemployment situation had been partially resolved in that one and a half million were dead and one million had emigrated. In 1858 a new movement arose – the Irish Republican Botherhood or Fenians, who were intent on getting England to grant their country independence. Gladstone eventually put through some liberal measures in 1869, disestablishing the Anglican church in Ireland. The following year he attempted to pass legislation to restrain the arbitrary expulsion of the tenantry.

Isaac Butt, an elderly Protestant from Ulster, considered that independence was the necessary requirement for improving the economy and so he founded the Home Rule League in 1870. Charles Parnell became its leader and headed the fight for autonomy until 1890 when he fell from favour with the masses. In 1879, following another bad harvest, Michael Davitt organised the Land League which made demands for security of tenure, free trade and moderate farm rents. Agricultural agitation was unleashed; demonstrations against the systematic evictions of tenants by their landlords took place. In 1893 the Home Rule Bill was passed by the House of Commons, but then rejected by the House of Lords. In the same year the Gaelic League was founded to revive interest in the Irish language and Irish literature.

The *Sinn Fein* (We Ourselves) Republican movement created by Arthur Griffith, demanded the immediate formation of a national parliament in 1905; there should be no half-measures, no semi-independence. Home Rule was finally granted in 1912 and was to be enforced two years later. But the Protestant Ulster Unionists strongly objected and bloody troubles fermented when Edward Carson founded the Ulster Volunteers that were immediately opposed by the Republican Irish Volunteers. The regular army refused to march against the Unionists and so the English government reached stalemate. Civil war was threatening when the First World War broke out.

During the war years *Sinn Fein* took over from the old parliamentary party. In April 1916 they proclaimed a republic in Dublin. From the time of this bloody Easter 1916 rising (when more than 500 died and 2500 nationalists were imprisoned) *Sinn Fein* gave up trying to take legal action. Supported by public opinion their goal was now independence at any price and by any means. Eamon De Valera became president of Sinn Fein and the Irish Volunteers in 1917. Two years later he was elected president of the 'Irish Republic' by *Sinn Fein* and the 'Irish Assembly'. English government in Ireland ground to a halt. More than a million armed Protestants were grouped in the north to resist invasion from the Irish Volunteers. A solution was envisaged in a political division of Ireland into two. Southern Ireland would obtain independence and Dominion status: Northern Ireland was to remain part of the United Kingdom. This arbitrary division, decided upon in an atmosphere of violent passions, unhappily satisfied neither Ulster (where Protestants and Catholics were enemy 'brothers') nor Southern Ireland which wanted independence for the whole country. But partition was instituted and the 1920 Government of Ireland Act separated the six counties in the north from the 26 counties in the south with a

Northern Ireland parliament set up in Belfast. On 6 December 1921 the Treaty of London created the Irish Free State. In 1922 this treaty, reluctantly accepted by the Nationalists, was rejected out of hand by the Republicans. For Ulster this meant the beginning of strife and enmity between the Protestant Unionists and the Catholic Nationalists, and in the south, civil war.

The Republican extremists in the Free State refused to accept their defeat and, by means of IRA (Irish Republican Army) activity, they gained control of large areas of the country. Murder, arson and violence grew. The insurrection reached Dublin and the city once again suffered from fire and bloodshed. Like all civil wars, the Irish war between supporters of the Irish Free State and those of the Republican movement was exceptionally unpleasant, dividing families, districts and towns 'degenerating into a kind of bloody folly, a spiral of crime, destruction and personal vengeance . . .' The war moved from Dublin to the provinces. Republican troops were driven back by regular soldiers from the urban centres they occupied: Limerick, Waterford, Cashel, Tipperary, Cork . . . The rebellion changed into guerrilla activity: attacks by bands of elusive men, ambushes, gun-battles, summary executions, explosions . . .

The death of Liam Lynch, the leader of the IRA in the Tipperary mountains, and the lack of arms and ammunition against a large and well-armed regular army, was to mark the beginnings of defeat. . . . On 27 May 1923 De Valera, president of the would-be Irish Republic appealed to his supporters to lay down their arms and give up the struggle. Officially the civil war was over. Ireland was physically and spiritually in ruins. Out of a total population of 2,750,000, 130,000 were unemployed and damages were estimated as 30 million pounds.

For Southern Ireland the period that followed, apart from a few crises, was one of pacification and reconstruction. The Cosgrave government faced difficulties over the question of Ulster, raised by James Craig. London maintained the border between the two 'countries' but the Irish debt to England stood at five million pounds. Cosgrave was attempting to modernise Ireland; consolidating central power to the detriment of local authority, reforming the judiciary, revitalising agriculture and encouraging foreign industrialists. In 1926 De Valera founded the official Republican party, *Fianna Fail* (the Warriors of Destiny), and took his seat in the *Dáil*. Southern Ireland was beginning to get back on its feet when one of the members of its government was assassinated in 1927. The murders were publicly disowned by the Republicans, but the Cosgrave government outlawed all revolutionary societies.

Opposed by De Valera, leader of the opposition, subjected to the economic crisis of 1929 and a target for renewed IRA activities, Cosgrave ceded power to De Valera in 1932. The latter governed until 1948. In the midst of this difficult situation and in an economic, social and political crisis, De Valera's objective remained the affirmation of the Free State's independence and the reuniting of Ulster. Economic warfare now broke out between England and Ireland and unemployment fermented social troubles; Communist groups grew up inside the IRA while the fascist 'Blue Shirt' group de-

veloped in the army. The government managed to keep these extremist elements in check and treaties to re-establish trade between Ireland and England were agreed in 1935. In 1937 De Valera took advantage of the political turmoil in England caused by the abdication of Edward VIII and presented a new constitution: Ireland would no longer be the Irish Free State but would be known as Eire; its people would no longer recognise the King of England and would be beholden to no-one but God. England accepted the constitution and a new step towards emancipation had been taken.

When the Second World War broke out Eire refused to participate, again demanded reunion with Ulster and protested when American troops landed in Northern Ireland in 1942. In spite of pressure by the United States Eire kept its policy of neutrality. The post-war period, therefore, was a prosperous one for Ireland with its strong currency reserves.

In the 1948 elections the *Fianna Fáil* (the Republican party) led by De Valera lost its absolute majority for the first time. John Costello, leader of the Conservative *Fine Gael* (the Irish Race) party, replaced De Valera. In April 1949 Eire proclaimed itself the Republic of Ireland and left the Commonwealth. For 11 years the rivalry of the parties *Fine Gael* and *Fianna Fáil* was to put a strain on the economic recovery of their country.

At the beginning of the sixties, under the stimulus of Sean Lamass, the young successor of De Valera, Ireland took on a new look. The younger generation, who had experienced neither the war of independence, nor the civil war, made light of the old quarrels. The new men who were in the key positions in Irish society were primarily concerned with efficiency in the economic and industrial fields. The old unchanging Ireland, seemingly unattracted by the lure of progress, became transformed in only a few years to the outward looking Republic of Ireland, with a totally different mentality.

The sad problem of Ulster still remains. The industrial north with its wealth of raw materials could undoubtedly complement the south with its essentially agriculturally-based economy. But is political cooperation in any sense practically possible? The Peace Movement started in 1976 by two Northern Irish women, Betty Williams and Mairead Corrigan, called for an end to the years of bloodshed and reunited thousands of men and women, Catholics and Protestants alike. Is this already a thing of the past? Or is it still possible to believe in the possibility that the two communities can work together? Is something that might happen tomorrow – or will it never happen?

THE THRIVING THEATRE

The English influence did not spare the Irish theatre and dramatic art, following the tried and tested formula of Congreve and Sheridan, confined itself to the light-hearted portrayal of a leisured and frivolous society, without bothering about the enormous source of inspiration that could have been drawn upon in reality. It was in this 'drawing-room comedy' tradition that the plays of Oscar Wilde were written (1854–1900). This leader of the Aesthetes was, in fact, Irish in origin only. Nor can the 'problem plays' of Bernard Shaw be considered as genuinely Irish. Shaw, who was born into the Anglo-Irish ruling class in Dublin, left the country at the age of 20. He is known as a rebel, but this is in terms only of his connection with the English theatre, where he used his genius and humour to sweep out the prevailing taste for romantic illusion.

It is amazing that a race as endowed with the gift of speech as the Irish waited so long for a national theatre. Up until the turn of the twentieth century, all efforts in this direction were in vain. And during the nineteenth century, the only dramatic author that Ireland can claim is Dion Boucicault (1822–90) who had a great success with his first play *London Assurance*. Melodrama has its devotees, but underneath the moonlight and ruined abbeys it conforms to a genre that ignores both Irish life and Irish literature. But in the wake of the foundation of the Gaelic League there was a sudden and extraordinary revival in the theatre.

The spirit behind this 'explosion' was the poet, William Butler Yeats (1865–1939). He founded the Irish Literary Society in London (in 1891) and the National Literature Society in Dublin in 1892; undertaking to create in Ireland 'a whole literature, a whole dramatic movement'. With its roots in ancient Celtic, the theatre could have only one religion – the worship of 'Beauty'. Everything dissolved into a dream and it was this dream that dramatic writing sought to translate into poetry. The union of the theatre and poetry (a union which had vanished with Dryden) revived from 1899 with the Irish Literary Theatre. Clustered around Yeats were his first disciples: Lady Gregory, a decisive influence in the poet's life; Edward Martyn, later the first president of Sinn Fein; George Moore, a great admirer of the free theatre of Antoine. These last two renounced the experiment at present underway: in the Literary Theatre action was subordinate to poetry and the denial of scenery and decoration ran counter to their taste for realism.

Yeats persevered in his enthusiasm for getting back to national tradition – even though the Dublin presentation of *The Countess Cathleen* in 1899 caused a storm of controversy (particularly among the clergy who regarded it as blasphemous). The Fay brothers joined him, then John Millington Synge (1871–1909) who was interested in the west of Ireland and produced six plays from his observations there – and, finally, Padraic Colum who, like the other members of the movement, wrote in English. This English usage was to cause factions among the Irish militants. The first play in Irish to reach the professional stage was *Casadh ant Sugain* by Douglas Hyde which in 1901 was performed with *Dairmuid and Grainne*, the fruit of the collaboration between Yeats and Moore.

The year 1903 was marked by Padraic Colum's *The Broken Soil*, Synge's *The Shadow of the Glen* and Yeats' *The Only Jealousy of Emer*. Lady Gregory created Irish comedy with short frenzied rhyming plays. In the middle of all this growth, Dublin's Abbey Theatre was born, thanks to the patronage of an Englishwoman, Miss Annie Frederica Hornim. She had the old Mechanic's Institute Theatre restored and allowed the group to use it from 1904, which they did successfully. Although Synge dominates the period, other authors, too, wrote for the Abbey Theatre, in Gaelic and in English; George FitzMaurice, Lennox Robinson, Seamus O'Kelly, Lord Dunsany . . . and so on. But this theatre-base was to play an essential part over and above its actual dramatic productions. Though it excluded political propaganda, it helped to reinforce nationalist feelings that were to inspire the uprising of 1916 and lead to the country's independence.

By the end of the civil war the Abbey Theatre had lost its innovating character. Yeats had emerged a little from his poetic dreaming and contours of reality were appearing in his work. Realism was the prerogative of Lennox Robinson and T. C. Murray; a realism that found its best interpreter in Sean O'Casey (1884–1965). Born in the slums of Dublin and moulded by Irish militants in the social upheaval, he brought revolt and distress to the

Brendan Behan.

stage through his remarkably powerful and disillusioned plays that brutally broke through the lyricism the public were accustomed to at the Abbey Theatre. 'I am going where life looks like life' one reads in *Juno and the Paycock* (1958).

Ireland's accession to independence and the rise of an influential clergy with a 'Puritan' outlook was to put a stop to this apogee of the Irish Theatre. Writers such as Denis Johnston, Seamus O'Kelly and Paul Vincent Carrol had to return to an inoffensive and melodramatic form of writing. Only the powerful plays of Brendhan Behan (1923–64) smacked of the scandalous; *The Quare Fellow*, *The Hostage* and, above all, *Borstal Boy*, adapted from his prison diary; the prison which he knew as an old member of the secret IRA, the banal and cruel, intense and carefree, picturesque and sordid life, death at the end of the road, were the main themes of his disturbing but essential work.

Other writers preferred to write in exile. As for the Abbey Theatre, it was destroyed in a fire in 1951 and was not revived until 15 years later, in July 1966, when its avant-garde role was only a memory.

Sean O'Casey.

IRISH ART

The art which developed in Ireland from the Stone Age to the arrival of the Anglo-Normans in the twelfth century can be defined by its amazing continuity and deep originality. Under foreign influences, though escaping Roman domination and the great barbaric invasions, Ireland, at the most western tip of Europe, remained in isolation which favoured the blossoming of an art stamped with mystery and showing a singular consistency over the centuries. The Irish tradition was disturbed from the ninth century by Viking raids and was blurred by the presence of the Norman invaders: from then on Irish art, bereft of its own identity, gradually allied itself to English art, of which it is, at times, nothing but a lifeless imitation, and it is often foreign artists who contribute to the national heritage.

Ireland's rich neolithic past is revealed by the numerous megalithic monuments. The Court Cairns in Ulster or in the north of Connacht, doubtless linked with fertility and prosperity cults, date back to the last quarter of the fourth millennium before Christ. Even more spectacular, on account of their size and architectural technique, are the Passage Graves in the Boyne valley, Newgrange, Knowth and Dowth: huge circular mounds at the heart of which are burial chambers covered with corbelled vaults, dating from about 2500 before Christ. The famous Newgrange tomb offers a complete range of Irish megalithic art, determined by the carved and sculpted decorations on the stones with their abstract ornamental designs of concentric circles, spirals and diamond-shapes. This repertoire of decoration is unprecedented and without equivalent in Europe, but has certain analogies with the later style of the Irish potters of the Bronze Age. The purpose of the simple raised monoliths in the form of a circle, found throughout the Bronze Age and in the early Iron Age, is obscure, but they mark the beginning of a long tradition, running from the megaliths to the huge carved crosses of the Christian era; passing through the commemorative stone pillars with their oghamic inscriptions (showing the first Irish alphabet, based on the Latin alphabet, and the earliest writing on the island), and the steles carved with a cross. The standing-stone is thus an integral part of the Irish countryside.

Bronze Age metalwork is represented by flat copper axes and various hammered gold ornaments (such as the lunulae, crescent-shaped necklaces finely decorated with geometric designs). The work of the first goldsmiths (often exported to Great Britain) took its place in a general movement peculiar to the development of Irish art: there was a permanence in the technical mastery shown by the craftsmen; skills handed down to the native goldsmiths until the twelfth century, and even found in the eighteenth century in the meticulous

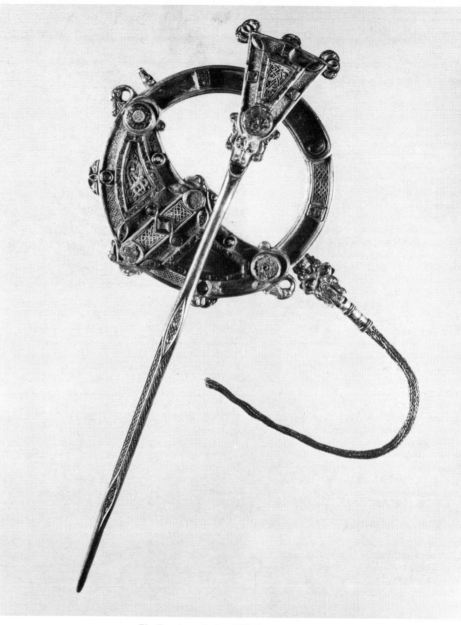

The Tara brooch circa 700 (National Museum of Ireland).

working of silver articles. Metalwork developed greatly after the arrival of the Celts. New types of tools and weapons appeared at the end of the Bronze Age. The Celtic invasion, wave after wave of it, made a deep impression on Ireland. Their influence really became obvious in the third and second centuries before Christ, when new metalworking techniques were introduced, together with an abstract and curvilinear style. This style (named after the La Tène civilisation in Switzerland) is typified by bronze articles decorated with engraving or in relief: bits, saddles, bridles, scabbards and so on, such as those found in Lisnacroghera in County Antrim. And also in gold articles: the gold collar found at Broighter and presently on show in the National Museum of Ireland is one of the most noteworthy examples. Strange cult stones and equally mysterious wood or stone sculptures also belong to primitive Celtic art; for instance, the Turoe stone, a phallic-looking pillar more than a

metre high and topped by a decorated dome in the abstract La Tène style. The human face is represented in the amazing three-faced head at Corleck and the double-faced heads on Boa Island in Lough Erne. Their significance is unknown. Pagan Irish art, that blossomed until the fifth century, remains a mystery in the absence of any documentary evidence. The Romantics, in particular, have spread a false and legendary image of the Irish Celts and their imaginary druids but, in reality, we know very little about primitive Celtic art. Although backward, insular and essentially abstract, this art was to survive until Christian times.

According to tradition, St Patrick arrived in Ireland in 432. But paganism was not really rooted out until the seventh century, after two hundred years of evangelisation, linked with considerable progress in monarchism. The first monasteries, collections of small wooden or dry-stone buildings, or sometimes even mud huts, are hardly worth attention for their architecture but, thanks to the intense activity they generated, they became great intellectual and artistic centres. The need for books was felt very swiftly. The Cathach, a psalter probably written at the beginning of the seventh century, is illuminated with letters whose decoration is borrowed from La Tène art; according to legend it was decorated by the hand of St Columba, the founder of the Scottish monastery of Iona in 563. The Irish monks were the originating force of a vast missionary movement, stretching to Scotland and thence to Northumbria in the north of England. Thus it was that contacts with foreigners were made and the resulting interchange of cultures enriched the pre-Christian Celtic tradition: evidence of this is the less backward and better quality manuscript of the Book of Durrow where Celtic interweaving mingles happily with elements of zoomorphic stylisation originating from Anglo-Saxon art. The foreign influence is also evident in the symbols of the Evangelists, which are inserted in this illustrated collection by means of only three colours – red, yellow and green. The Book of Durrow is the first of a line of sumptuous gospels that affirm the links between the Irish artists and those of Northumbria: the Book of Lindisfarne (in English), the Book of Lichfield, the Book of Armagh and the wonderful Book of Kells. The latter was undoubtedly begun in the monastery of Iona at the end of the eighth century and was finished in Kells at the beginning of the ninth century, after Iona had been sacked by the Vikings. The exuberance of the designs, the variety and minute details of the invention, the striking precision of the colours, all raise the calligraphic style and the illuminations to an almost 'baroque' level.

The eighth and ninth centuries were also the important period for goldsmithing and ornament akin to that in the manuscripts was used to decorate superb pieces that were worked with an exceptional technical skill: huge bronze basins (probably used as lamps), the Ardagh Chalice, a ciborium of repoussé silver, enhanced with gold filigree and *cloisonné* studs; the penannular Tara Brooch, of bronze studded with glass and amber; the gilded bronze plaque portraying a Crucifixion scene found in Athlone. This iconographic style, which until then was unusual in a decorative tradition which was essentially abstract and zoomorphic, appeared first on the stone High Crosses some three or four metres high. Simple carved steles were succeeded by very elaborate crosses, such as those of Ahenny, Moone, Kilkieran and Killamery, ornamented with very complex abstract or figure compositions. And, while the illuminated design declined following the Viking raids, sculpture still flourished and reached its culmination in the superb crosses of Durrow, Monasterboice and in the regal Cross of the Scriptures at Clonmacnoise. This period also saw the construction of churches, with high round towers behind them, acting as bell towers, but also as refuges to give protection from the invaders.

In the tenth century the new waves of attacks from the Norsemen put a stop to all artistic activity and it was not until the beginning of the eleventh century, in the reign of Brian Boru, that Ireland knew another creative period, now stamped also by the immovable Viking presence in Dublin, Wexford, Waterford, Cork and Limerick. Thus the Norwegian style was applied in Irish metalwork –

The Golden Choker from Glenisheen, circa 800 BC (National Museum of Ireland).

crosses, shrines and book-covers of the eleventh and twelfth centuries show a pleasing mixture of Celtic and Scandinavian styles, particularly evident in the Shrine of St Patrick's Bell, decorated with long serpents. Among the best artefacts of the period are the Cross of Clonmacnoise, the Cross of Cong and the Reliquary of St Manchan.

The Irish church survived until the beginning of the twelfth century without any form of hierarchy, but was then organised according to the European system and divided into dioceses. This new structure increased the authority of the bishops whose growing power was illustrated by the crosses that henceforth bore their effigies. A number of religious buildings were erected but, since they conformed to the traditional Irish architecture, they were small and very plain. The majority of Romanesque churches were made up of a simple rectangular nave with a square east-facing chancel. But there was an important innovation – the introduction of sculptured decoration on the exterior portals and on the chancel arches. Cormac's Chapel at Cashel, the 'Nun's Church' at Clonmacnoise and the latest-dating church at Clonfert, which are among the most beautiful Irish Romanesque buildings, show an interesting form of ornamentation in which the specifically indigenous designs, interlaced and fretted, are lost amid a profusion of decorations inspired by foreign designs from England, Germany, Saintonge and Poitou.

The establishment of new monastic orders, favoured by the reform of the Irish church, made a big contribution to enlarging the horizons. A new monastic lifestyle arose, especially with the Cistercians, and a different conception of religious architecture. Their introduction into Ireland was due to the initiative of St Malachy, Primate of Armagh, and friend of St Bernard. He founded the Abbey of Mellifont, consecrated in 1157, after spending some time in Clairvaux. The church at Mellifont must have been a great surprise for the Irish who had always refused to undertake large-scale building; it is 60 metres long and follows the plan of a basilica. Give or take a few modifications, the monasteries, such as Baltinglass, Boyle and Jerpoint (to name only the principal ones), were now built according to the general plan adopted by the Order of St Bernard, as today's ruins testify. However the rule forbidding any kind of decoration was not enforced very strictly in Ireland. There are even curious traditional designs decorating the capitals at Jerpoint and Baltinglass; the last traces of local colour to be expressed in Irish art, which was gradually being reduced to nothing by the Anglicising politics of the new invaders.

With the coming of the Anglo-Normans, whose first expedition was mounted in 1169, and who had

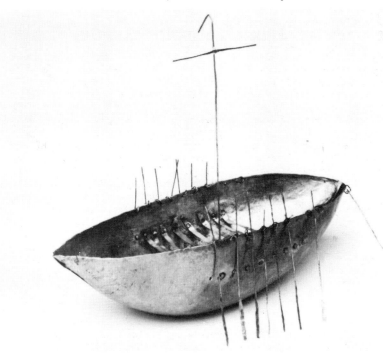

The golden boat from Broighter (County Londonderry), first century (National Museum of Ireland).

control over three-quarters of the country by the middle of the thirteenth century, the end of the Middle Ages was marked by the building of impressive fortified castles, such as those at Trim and Roscommon; of stone-built bridges (previously they were built of wood); and of churches built to new dimensions. The two huge cathedrals in Dublin, Christ Church and St Patrick's, are reflections of their English gothic models. Only a number of sculptures remain untouched by this degenerate gothic style; the Butler family tombs in Kilkenny Cathedral and the Gowran Collegiate Church still show true originality.

The only real artistic centres disappeared in the sixteenth century when the monasteries were mostly suppressed. Hereafter the situation was made worse by wars and political and social troubles. It was only at the beginning of the eighteenth century that conditions improved enough to allow artistic talent to bloom again – at least in the ruling Anglo-Irish aristocracy. The principles of Palladio were fashionable in Dublin, where public buildings and private houses were built in this style. It was also fashionable around 1750 to commission rococo stuccowork, an exuberant form of decoration that only came to the fore once, and which lost favour after the victory of neo-classicism at the end of the century. Georgian Ireland, which saw the building and extending of cities to give them their present appearance, adopted the English styles of the day.

The renewal of nationalism in the nineteenth century had a marked effect on the decorative arts – particularly in stained-glass work; the windows in St Patrick's Church at Jordanstown, executed in 1870, were inspired by the illuminations in the Book of Durrow. The revival of the plastic arts, especially painting, did not make itself felt until the twentieth century, under the influence of the artist Jack B. Yeats, who played an important role in the cultural activity of his country.

FROM ONE PUB – TO ANOTHER

Ireland is a country of a thousand secrets and as many of these can be guessed at in the lively atmosphere of its public houses as during a string of leisurely walks in its verdant countryside. Have you never gone into a dark, throbbing pub* in Dublin, one of those places where women used to be separated from the 'drinkers', segregated in a small room that had a serving hatch opening into the bar? Have you never been in an old village cafe that also serves as a grocer's and carries the name of its proprietor over the door? Irish life snugly shuts itself away in places like these in order to pontificate over pints of stout or several glasses of whiskey. For though the islander is virtually indifferent about good food, he has a definite inclination to drink: a great deal is consumed here – 126 litres of beer per head each year. This inclination is partly due to the quality of the national beverages.

Beer is undeniably the greatest of these, or to be more precise, the bitter stout or 'black' beer. Ireland exports some 40 per cent of its total beer production and more than half is stout. In the EEC export tables Ireland is on a par with Germany and the greatest portion of its stout – Guinness – is destined for neighbouring Great Britain. Guinness? A name of international repute. About five million bottles a day are produced in the brewery founded by Arthur Guinness in 1759. At the end of the last century this brewery, based in Dublin on the banks of the Liffey, was the largest in the world; today it is the largest in Europe, and employs nearly 4000 workers. There are those who claim that Guinness Extra Stout is incomparable when it is drunk in Ireland – either bottled or draught. Doubtless the purity of the spring waters from the Wicklow hills, used in the brewing, contribute to improving the flavour of this highly fermented beer which has a 5 per cent alcoholic content. But the main reason is because stout, with its singularly bitter taste, is never pasteurised here – though outside Ireland it may be (as draught Guinness is in Great Britain).

Though Guinness reigns supreme in Dublin pubs, two other brands of stout take precedence in Cork. The James J. Murphy & Co. Ltd. Brewery, founded in 1883, produces a pasteurised beer, milder than Guinness, while Beamish and Crawford Ltd. (dating back to 1879) also produce a pasteurised beer very like Guinness but of a lighter colour and with a whiter head.

Because these stouts (whose density reaches 1039/1040) predominate, one tends to forget sometimes that Ireland also brews other beers, namely

*Pubs are open here from 10.00 to 23.00 or 23.30, with a break from 14.30 to 15.30 – 'the holy hour' as it is called in Dublin, where it is claimed that this is done so that the parish priest can drink his beer in peace!

ales and lagers. Ale, a highly fermented beer, with a density around 1036, generally coppery in colour, though sometimes darker, is gaining in popularity on the island. 'Time' ale is no longer to be found and the little Friary Hill brewery at Enniscorthy (County Wexford) stopped manufacturing in 1956, conferring its licence on Pelforth, a French brewery, to produce its Ruby Ale; but several types of ale are still in existence today. Among those who brew it are E. Smithwick and Sons Ltd., founded in Kilkenny in 1710, who make a sweetish beer generally sold on draught; Macardle Moore and Co. Ltd. whose beer is brewed in Dundalk and is distinguished by its darker colouring and dry aroma; Phoenix, in Waterford, who produce a bitter ale, sold only in bottles. But perhaps you prefer lager, a low fermentation beer gaining in popularity? Beamish and Crawford Ltd. and Guinness have created lagers of densities ranging between 1039 and 1042.

There is only one alcohol sufficiently noble to rival these stouts, ales and lagers, which catch at the throat and fill the heart with gladness – whiskey.* Not Scotch, nor bourbon – the Irish will not tolerate any confusion! – true whiskey was born in Ireland. It is true that Scotland claims to have invented the authentic whisky, but in Ireland they are more inclined to attribute the first distillation to St Patrick – he taught the Irish monks the secret art of distilling, which he had learned in the course of his travels, and it was from Ireland that the secret was indirectly spread to Scotland by the religious missionaries. Whatever the uncertainty of its origins, whiskey is the best in the world – almost everyone agrees with this!

The arrival of the present flavour, though, is a long story. It appears that during the eleventh century an alcohol that foreshadowed whiskey was made out of fermented barley pulp; this was usquebaugh, much appreciated by the Norman invaders in 1170. During the Elizabethan times this Irish alcohol was very highly thought of in England and countless casks of it were sent over. And from then on, in spite of the vicissitudes of history that had a deep effect on the island, whiskey pursued its brilliant career. There were a thousand or so distilleries in the country in the eighteenth century. At the beginning of the twentieth century Ireland sent the greatest amount of its drink production to the United States but Prohibition interrupted this export and when it began again later it was with less intensity. Today Ireland sends only a quarter of its production abroad.

Since 1966 there has been only one national manufacturer of whiskey – Irish Distillers Ltd. whose headquarters are in Dublin. It was formed from the amalgamation of four companies who, up until then, had shared ownership of the distilleries: John Jameson and Sons Ltd., founded in Bow Street in 1780 by the son-in-law of John Haig (another of the great names in whisky) – this was one of the first firms to perfect the manufacturing technique; John Power and Son Ltd. founded in 1791 in John's Lane by Sir John Power, High Sheriff of Dublin; and two lesser companies, Cork Distilleries Co. Ltd. and Tullamore Dew Ltd.

The exquisite taste of Irish whiskey is dependent

*The spelling 'whiskey' differentiates the Irish spirit from Scotch whisky, though it is worth noting that the Irish themselves have long dropped the 'e' in general usage.

on the proportion of cereals used; obviously a well-kept secret but it is known that it is made from about 50 per cent of malted barley (germinated), 30 per cent of non-malted barley, 10 per cent of oats and as much corn and rye. The barley, most of which is Irish in origin, is first dried to reduce its humidity level to 12 per cent for the barley that is to be malted and to 6 per cent for the barley that is not to be malted. After the barley is germinated, the various cereals are mixed and pulverised in the traditional manner, by huge grindstones; only the oats are merely crushed. The brewing is then done in the same way as it is in Scotland: drenched in warm water the grain is transformed, by the conversion of its starches, into a rich sugar solution called wort: to this is added yeast and then it is left for three or four days in gigantic fermentation vats (containing up to 33,000 gallons). When fermentation is finished, the impure alcohol obtained (about 8 per cent pure alcohol) is distilled in copper stills which are heated simultaneously by a naked flame and by steam pipes. These kettles too are enormous – an Irish wash still can contain some 25,000 gallons (compared to only 5000 in Scotland). Another difference between the Irish whiskey and its Scottish rival is that here the whiskey is distilled three times, not twice. During the course of each distilling only the second third part is retained, the first and third being distilled again.

The whiskey obtained by this alchemy is put into oak casks and left in cellars for a period varying from seven to fifteen years, and even longer. It is during this ageing process that the alcohol acquires its own flavour, because of the type of cask in which it is stored; some barrels are new, others have been 'smoked', and still others have previously contained sherry, port, rum or even whiskey. At the end of this stay in casks the whiskey is blended; mixed with whiskies from the same distillery but of different ages and from different barrels. It is not, then, the same as the Scottish blending, where whiskies from different distilleries are mixed; the result stays a 'single'. Then comes the final phase – bottling. Water is added to give the required alcoholic strength and the whiskey is 'imprisoned' in bottles that have been cleaned with compressed air. From that moment on it is ready to be drunk.

And how you drink it is important too! In little tots, neat, with an equal amount of fresh water or, as John Jameson advises, 'on the rocks' (four or five centilitres of whiskey on ice cubes). Or you can choose the celebrated Irish coffee, invented just after the last war by a barman at Shannon Airport. Put some crystallised brown sugar into a lightly warmed glass, pour on whiskey until the glass is a third full. Stir well and then fill the glass with strong hot black coffee up to two centimetres below the rim. Complete the potion with a layer of whipped (or fresh) cream, that must stay on the top. Then drink it, allowing the whiskey to filter through the cream. John Power advocates putting the sugar in after the whiskey and the coffee, Jameson is a sugar-coffee-whiskey man. But, in fact, whatever method you use, the main thing is not to be stingy with the whiskey!

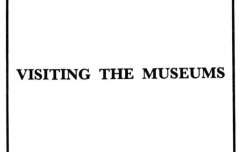

VISITING THE MUSEUMS

Lovers of vast and changing skies, of gentle hills, steep cliffs and jagged coastlines, find the Emerald Isle a delightful paradise, where the sheer spectacle of nature is an ever-present delight. But are they aware that visiting the wonderful museums here can also be a pleasurable and not incompatible activity? If they spare the time visitors can take back very different, but equally superb, memories from these.

And so a short stay in Dublin is a 'must'. The National Museum of Ireland contains the most important collection of mediaeval Irish antiquities and art. It is also a showcase of native goldsmithing with its beautiful collection of gold Celtic ornaments, fibulae and lunulae, dating from the Bronze Age, and the real gems of the high Middle Ages such as the Ardagh Chalice and the Tara Brooch, or the Moylough Belt-shrine. No less remarkable are the twelfth century religious treasures, the Lismore and Inisfallen crosses, the famous Cross of Cong and the Shrine of St Patrick's Bell. This panoramic view of Irish goldsmithing is completed by the twentieth century exhibits in the museum's contemporary crafts' section.

There are also paintings very well worth seeing in Dublin. The main European schools are represented in the National Gallery of Ireland, augmented by an impressive collection of fifteenth century Novgorod icons. Among the best paintings are Cranach's *Judith with the head of Holophernes*, Van der Weyden's *St Luke painting the Virgin* and Titian's *Portrait of Baldassare Castiglione*. A room is also devoted to Jack B. Yeats, brother of the poet and considered to be the greatest of contemporary Irish painters. Many of his works are also on show in the Municipal Gallery of Modern Art. A private collector, Sir Hugh Lane, was the moving force behind this museum, which has been housed in Charlemont House since 1933. He wanted to make a donation to the town where he was born, but could not find a sufficiently dignified setting for his works of art in Dublin; and so he shared his collection between London's National Gallery and a small room in Harcourt Street, where the first modern art gallery in the British Isles was opened in 1908. On his death the two museums started a law suit and this was resolved by arbitration in 1959: the pictures were divided into two lots and are displayed alternately in Dublin and London on a five year exchange basis. This impressive 'split' collection is mainly composed of nineteenth century French canvases, particular by the Impressionists; including, among other riches, Corot's *Palace of the Popes at Avignon*, Renoir's *Les Parapluies* and Manet's *Portrait of Eva Gonzales* and *Music at the Tuileries*.

There should be no question of leaving Dublin without looking at its impressive libraries. Trinity College Library possesses a most admirable collection of Irish manuscripts and early printed books – the Book of Durrow, the Book of Armagh (which includes the only extant copy of the New Testament in Ireland and a collection of texts by St Patrick) and, above all, the Book of Kells, a new page of which is displayed each day. These are the most eloquent evidence of the magnificent illumination achieved from the seventh to the ninth centuries. If your interest is in foreign miniatures, from the continent, or the East, and the Far-East, then you must certainly visit the Chester Beatty Library, housing an amazing and tasteful collection created by this American millionaire. On display are Babylonian clay tablets, Egyptian and Greek papyri, dazzling Persian and Indian miniatures, as well as a number of European manuscripts, including a Book of the Hours by the Duc de Berry and a prayer book once belonging to Philip II of Spain.

In Northern Ireland you should not miss the Ulster Museum and Art Gallery in Belfast which, as well as sections devoted to history and regional archaeology, has an interesting collection of pictures with works by Brueghel, Velours, Turner and Lawrence. But the museum's prize exhibit is the Girona Treasure, discovered in 1968 off the north coast of County Antrim. Jewellery and gold and silver coins were among the finds in the remains of this Spanish galleon which sank after the 'invincible' Armada was defeated.

A much later innovation is one that can really be appreciated in this country of strong traditions – the ethnographic museums. Such is the Ulster Folk Museum, eight miles from Belfast. It is an open-air museum, like those at Glencolumbkille in Donegal and Bunratty (County Clare) in Eire. These Folk Museums are reconstructions of the picturesque village with its traditional houses and workshops, illustrating, in an original and pleasant fashion for the visitor, the life of the Irish peasantry at different periods in history.

INDEX

PHOTOGRAPHS